Diana

Raising Dough

Bloomington Board of REALTORS®

authorHOUSE®

AuthorHouse™
1663 Liberty Drive, Suite 200
Bloomington, IN 47403
www.authorhouse.com
Phone: 1-800-839-8640

©2008 Bloomington Board of REALTORS®. All rights reserved.

No part of this book may be reproduced, stored in a retrieval system, or transmitted by any means without the written permission of the author.

First published by AuthorHouse 10/23/2008

ISBN: 978-1-4389-2140-2 (sc)

ISBN: 978-1-4389-2140-2 (sc)

Printed in the United States of America
Bloomington, Indiana

This book is printed on acid-free paper.

Feeding Kids in Monroe and Owen
County Of Bloomington, Indiana
A Collection of Recipes
by The Bloomington Board of
REALTORS
And Friends

FOREWORD

Bloomington Board of REALTORS® "Food Drive Committee" from 2002 -2008 has been very involved in the Community Kitchen of Monroe County, Indiana. Not only have we volunteered our time with feeding the hungry we have gone into the community of Bloomington, Indiana, and have asked for help in feeding children with the Community Kitchen summer program. The restaurants that have joined us in feeding the kids in the summer are Lennie's, Michael's Uptown Café, and Tutto Bene Wine Café.

The Community Kitchen delivery van serves over 10,000 sack breakfasts to low-income children at designated sites, and the numbers are growing larger each year. Each breakfast has four items selected from three categories - grain, dairy, and fruit. The breakfasts contain such things as boxed juice, cereal, cereal bars, granola, fruit, and yogurt cups. The area neighborhoods that have been involved with this program are delighted with the summer program "Feed the Kids". Each year we earn more money from members of the Bloomington Board of REALTORS® and the local community restaurants.

In 2007-2008 the Food Drive Committee designed this lovely cookbook to help serve a larger group to help feed the children of Monroe and Owen Counties in Indiana. From the Bloomington Board of REALTORS® – Food Drive Community we want to thank you for helping us reach our goal that no child goes hungry.

ACKNOWLEDGEMENT

On behalf of the Bloomington Board of REALTORS®, we are proud to bring you this collection of great recipes. The Bloomington Board of REALTORS® Food Drive Committee has worked long and hard to develop something that will help feed children in our community.

This cookbook is dedicated to all children who have gone to bed hungry. This is our way of saying you have not been forgotten. We hope by publishing this cookbook, children in need will find the world a better place. Our goal is to work for the Monroe County Community Kitchen in Bloomington, Indiana and for other organizations that help feed children. We hope that with the purchase of this cookbook, another child will be fed through the dedication and love that the Bloomington Board of REALTORS® Food Drive Committee has published.

On this occasion we would like to thank members of the cookbook committee for all their hard work and give a special thanks to all of the REALTORS® and friends that donated their favorite recipes. It is with their help that this cookbook was possible.

Thanks to all of you! Much effort was made to make this collection of favorite recipes friendly and error free. We do apologize for any error we may have made and hope they are few.

Please enjoy the cookbook and all the wonderful meals you will be making.

All proceeds of this cookbook will help feed children of Monroe and Owen Counties in Indiana.

Darlene Cook, Co-Chairperson
Shauna Williams, Co-Chairperson
Linda Kidwell, Cookbook Coordinator
Barbara Joseph
Shannon Passwaiter
Laryn M. Pfrommer
Shelley Puckett
Faye Jameson, Staff

Table of contents

FOREWORD
ACKNOWLEDGEMENT
Appetizers & Beverages

Artichokes with Red Bell Pepper Aioli	2
Bacon Cheese Mini Appetizers	3
Black Bean, Hearts of Palm & Corn Salsa	4
Chap Bap Ran Vietnamese Corn and Coconut Fritters	5
Cheese Stuffed Mushrooms	6
Cheese and Crab Stuffed Mushrooms	7
Cheese Wafers	8
Chicken Pastry Squares	9
Cocktail Meatballs	10
Corn and Black Bean Tortilla Cakes	11
Cream Cheese Ball	12
Deviled Eggs	12
Easy Artichoke Dip	13
Elegant Meat Balls	14
Fresh Salsa	15
Fresh Salsa	15
Guacamole	16
Guacamole Dip	16
Hot Artichoke Dip	17
Hot Cocoa Mix	17
Hot Corn Dip	18
Hot Crab Dip	19
Hot Ham & Cheese Spread	19
Hot Spinach Artichoke Dip	20
Italian Spritz	20
Jessica's Spin Dip	21
Little Smokie Stogies	22
Orange Julius	22
Provolone Terrine Recipe	23
Rosemary Party Nuts	25
Rye Babies	25
Sausage Balls	26
Seven Layer Dip	26
Simple Tofu Bites	27
Spiced Pork Meatballs with Guacamole	28
Spinach and Artichoke Dip	29
Spinach-Artichoke Dip	30
Spinach & Sausage Stuffed Mushrooms	31
Tex Mex Dip	32
Tortilla Roll-ups	33

Uncle John's Cajun Wings	34
Zucchini Fritters	35

Breads

Angel Biscuits	38
Apple Bread	39
Banana Sour Cream Coffee Cake	40
Corn Cake	41
Cranberry Bread	41
Fabulous French Toast Casserole	42
Fantastic Pecan Rolls	43
Grandma J's B-Bread	44
Joan's Delish Apple Bread	45
Monkey Bread	46
One Egg Banana Nut Bread	46
Pumpkin Bread	47
Pumpkin Bread	48
Pumpkin Bread	49
Rise & Shine Biscuits	49
Warm Stuffed Cheesy Bread	50
Zucchini Bread	50

Casseroles, Veggies, & Sides

Aunt Ginny's Delight	52
Baked Beans	52
Breakfast Casserole	53
Broccoli Casserole	53
Corn Casserole	54
Cabbage & Rice Casserole	54
Cheesy Chicken Nugget Casserole	55
Cheesy Potato Casserole	55
Cheesy Taco Bake	56
Chicken Casserole	57
Corn Pudding	57
Drunken Green Beans	58
Gourmet Baked Beans	59
Hash Brown Casserole	60
Hearty Breakfast Custard Casserole	61
Porter's Slop	62
Sausage Casserole	62
Sautéed Green Beans	63
Seafood Casserole	64
Turkey Tetrazzini Casserole	64
Veggie Chili	65
Yuma Seta	66

Cookies & Candies

Brownies	68

Chocolate Popcorn	69
Easy Mint Delights	69
Gooey Brownies	70
Mississippi Mud	71
My Mom's Brazil Nut Sticks	72
No-bake Chocolate Oatmeal Cookies	72
Oatmeal Cookies	73
Old Fashioned Sugar Cookies	74
Peanut Butter Fingers	75
Peanut Butter Fudge	76
Porcupine Cookies	77
Raspberry Danish Dessert	78
Shortening Sugar Cookies	79
Snicker doodles	79
Sugar Bars	80
Sweet-Heat Almonds	81
White Cookies	82

International Recipes

Baba Ganouj	84
Birouats	85
Cheesy Chicken Enchiladas	**86**
Chicken Enchilada Ring	87
Chiles Rellenos	88
Easy Beef Enchiladas	89
Eggplant Parmesan	90
Hungarian Goulash	91
Italian Beef Stew	92
Lebanese Spinach and Rice	93
Muc Nhoi (Vietnamese Stuffed Squid)	94
Ginger Lime Dipping Sauce	95
Pollo en Mole Rojo Sencillo	96
Pollo En Mole Verde (Chicken in Green Mole)	97
Shrimp Scampi	98
Tabhouleh (The Real Thing) Lebanese Garden Wheat Salad	**99**

Meat, Poultry, Fish

Chicken Cacciatore	103
Chicken Cordon Bleu	104
Chicken Stew	105
Cornish Game Hens with Wild Rice	106
Holiday Cranberry Chicken	106
Hot Chicken Salad	107
Lasagna	108
Maryland Crab Cakes	109
Meat Loaf	109

Miso-Marinated Sea Bass	110
Sloppy Joes	110
Southern Style Deep Fried Chicken	111
Stuffed Green Peppers	112
Texas Pot Roast	113
Venison Tenderloin	114

Pastries, Desserts, Cakes & Frosting

Cake Dough Peach Dessert	117
Caramel Apple Cake	118
Cheesecake(s)	119
Chocolate Fudge or Icing	120
Chocolate Glaze	120
Clafouti	121
Crisco Pie Crust	**122**
Crock Pot Cake	123
Derby Pie	123
Divine Apple Strudel	124
English Coffee Cake	125
European Fudge Sauce	125
Grand Marnier Chocolate Cake	126
Green Slime Dessert	127
Joan's Coffee Cake	128
Miracle Whip Cake	129
Moist and Easy Cookie Sheet Chocolate Cake	130
My Favorite Chocolate Frosting	131
One Egg Cake	131
Pineapple Carrot Cake	132
Poppy Seed Cake	133
Pumpkin Spice Cake	134
Strawberry Pie	135
Strawberry Pizza	136
Tami's Praline-Pumpkin Cake	137
Turtle Brownies	138
Velvet Frosting	139
Vermont Maple Walnut Pie	139
Walnut Carrot Cake	140
Weinerbrod Danish Pastry	141
Yummy Quick Chocolate Cake	142
Yummy Quick Chocolate Cake Icing	142

Soups, Salads, & Sauces

Asian Cole Slaw Salad	144
BBQ Sauce	145
Bean Salad	**145**
Broccoli Cauliflower Salad	146
Broccoli Slaw Salad	147

Chicken and Hominy Soup (Posole')	148
Chicken Noodle Soup	149
Chili	150
Crab Salad	150
Cranberry Salad	151
Egg Salad	151
Gazpacho	152
Great Split Pea Soup	152
Lentil Vegetable Soup	153
Lemon Chicken Artichoke Soup	154
Mandarin Almond Spinach Salad	155
Mandarin Orange Salad	156
Meat Marinade	156
Oriental Cabbage Crunch Salad	157
Pat's Ham and Bean Soup	158
Potato Salad	158
Potato Soup	159
Salsa Cruda	159
Salsa Ranchera	160
Salsa Verde	160
Sesame Dressing	161
Spaghetti Sauce	162
Sweet – Savory Salad	163
Tuna Salad	164
Tuna Salad	164
Vegetable Soup	165
Veggie Chili	166
Wanda's Cranberry Sauce Extraordinaire	167

The Perfect Kitchen

Appetizers & Beverages

Artichokes with Red Bell Pepper Aioli

Trim the points and stems from 6 lg. artichokes. Rub the cut surfaces with lemon juice. Then steam 35-45 minutes or wrap each artichoke individually in plastic wrap and microwave each artichoke approximately 6 minutes. Cool.

When the artichokes are cool enough to handle remove the leaves and arrange in concentric circles on a round platter(s) Reserve the hearts for your own use. Leave a space for a bowl in the middle of the platter. Chill until ready to serve.

Make the aioli:
8 garlic cloves (you can roast them for a milder flavor)
2 roasted and peeled red bell peppers
2 c. real mayonnaise
Salt and pepper to taste ¼ tsp. cayenne pepper.
Combine all in the work bowl of a food processor fitted with the steel blade and puree.

Refrigerate well covered until needed then divide between the bowls on the platters and serve. (Sauce will keep 5 days refrigerated-cover tightly it is really pungent)

Candace Grover

Bacon Cheese Mini Appetizers

Makes 24 appetizers

1   10 oz Can Flaky Biscuits
1   8 oz Pkg Cream Cheese (Near room temperature)
2   Tbsp Milk
1   Jar "Real Bacon Bits" or 8-10 Slices Crispy Bacon
1   Small Onion Finely Chopped
1/2 c Real Parmesan Cheese Grated
2   Tbsp Chopped Fresh Parsley

Preheat oven to 375 degrees. Using the Food Chopper, dice onion and chop the fresh parsley. Grate the fresh parmesan cheese. Place cream cheese, milk, onion, parsley, bacon bits and grated cheese in the Batter Bowl. Mix well using the Mix 'n scraper.

Separate flaky biscuits into layers. Place layers over cup of mini muffin pan. Dredge the mini tart shaper in flour and press biscuit into each cup. Using small scoop, place 1 scoop of cream cheese mixture into each biscuit. Bake 12-15 minutes.

Connie Rautenkranz

Black Bean, Hearts of Palm & Corn Salsa

Makes about 5 cups.

1 16-oz can black beans, rinsed & drained
1 10-oz can whole kernel corn, drained
1 7 1/2-oz can hearts of palm, drained, cut into 1/4 inch thick rounds
1 10-oz can diced tomatoes, drained
1/2 minced red onion
1/2 c chopped fresh cilantro
1/4 c olive oil
3 Tbsp fresh lime juice
1 tsp ground coriander

Mix all ingredients in medium bowl. Season to taste with salt & pepper. Can be prepared 1 day ahead. Cover and refrigerate. Good with taco chips.

Rachel LaGrange

Chap Bap Ran
Vietnamese Corn and Coconut Fritters

1.c fresh or frozen corn, if frozen do not defrost
¼ coconut cream, taken from the top of an unshaken can of coconut milk. Available at local Asian groceries
1 egg lightly beaten
1/3 c all-purpose flour
1 ½ tsp. cornstarch
½ tsp. salt
½ tsp. sugar
Dipping Sauce
2 Tbsp. Huy Fong Siracha sauce, available widely in most grocery stores and Asian markets
2 tsp. water
1 tsp. sugar
Corn or Canola oil for frying

Place the corn in a work bowl of a food processor and pulse about 12-15 times, pausing to scrape down the bowl occasionally. You want it to sort of stick together when pinched together.

Transfer the corn to a bowl and then add the coconut cream, flour, cornstarch, salt and sugar. Mix to combine. The batter should be fairly thick. If it is too thin add a little more flour, up to 1 Tbsp set batter aside to rest 30 minutes.

Make the dipping sauce while the batter rests. Combine dipping sauce ingredients in a small bowl. Taste for heat. If it is too spicy add additional sugar and water.

Heat a wok or 5 qt. dutch oven and add oil to a depth of 1". Bring the oil to 350 degrees. Then scoop up about 2 tsp. of the fritter batter and slip into the hot oil. They should be about 1 ½" in diameter. Do not crowd the pan. Fry turning once until golden and puffed then drain on a rack and keep warm in a low oven until all are cooked. If they deflate or do not puff they need to cook a little longer.

Arrange on a plate with the dipping sauce and garnish with some sprigs of fresh mint

Candace Grover

Cheese Stuffed Mushrooms

2 lbs large button mushrooms
1/2 c grated Parmesan Cheese
1 c finely chopped or grated onion
2 - 3 cloves garlic, finely chopped
Salt and ground pepper to taste
½ tsp. ground oregano
3 Tbsp chopped fresh parsley
3/4 c virgin olive oil
1/2 c dry bread crumbs

Preheat oven to 350 degrees

Wash mushrooms, remove stems and finely chop them.   Mix stems with cheese, breadcrumbs, onion, garlic, parsley, oregano, salt & pepper. Pour 1/3 cup oil into baking pan and spread over the bottom. Placed stuffed mushrooms into pan. If there is left over stuffing, spread around mushrooms in pan. Pour remaining oil over each mushroom and any extra stuffing.   Bake on middle rack in 350 degrees oven for about 25 minutes.   SERVES 6 to 8 PEOPLE

Mary Gajewski

Cheese and Crab Stuffed Mushrooms

1 lb. Fresh mushrooms
2 Tbsp onion, chopped
2 Tbsp butter
¼ c soft bread cubes
¼ c crab, finely chopped
½ tsp salt
2 tsp lemon juice
¼ tsp Worcestershire sauce
½ c white wine (or cooking sherry)
½ c shredded cheddar cheese.

Remove stems from mushrooms and set caps aside; chop stems. In small skillet, sauté onion and chopped stems in butter until tender. Add bread cubes and crab; cook over medium heat, stirring constantly until lightly brown. Add salt, lemon juice and Worcestershire sauce. Fill mushroom caps with bread stuffing. Place in 9 inch square or shallow baking dish. Pour wine around caps. Bake for 15 minutes. Top with cheese. Continue baking 8 to 10 minutes until cheese melts.

Faye Jameson

Cheese Wafers

The true name of these things is "Idiot's Cheese Delights" probably because they are so easy to make.

1 c butter at room temperature
4 c shredded sharp cheddar cheese
1 tsp. Worcestershire sauce
1/4 tsp. cayenne (red) pepper
1 c flour
1/4 c lightly toasted sesame seeds (optional)

If using sesame seeds lightly toast in a skillet stirring constantly until just slightly colored. They will deepen slightly in color as they cool, remove from heat and set aside. Mix the butter, cheese, cayenne pepper and Worcestershire sauce together well (I use the paddle on a Kitchen Aid stand mixer to do this, but it can be done by hand). When well combined start adding the flour 1/2 C. at a time. When all of the flour has been incorporated into the dough, divide the dough into 3 even pieces. Roll each section of dough into a log about the size of the tube in a roll of paper towels. Wrap well in plastic and chill for several hours. (The dough can be frozen at this point and held for about 3 months.) When well chilled and firm, slice in to 1/4" thick rounds. If you are using the sesame seeds dip each round into the sesame seeds and then place on the baking sheet. Bake at 350 degrees for about 15 min. or until golden brown.

If you have frozen the dough, just slice it as above and bake. No need to thaw first. I've also thought they might be good with Gruyere Cheese and maybe some caraway seed. I don't think I'd put the caraway on top but maybe work some into the dough.

Candace Grover

Chicken Pastry Squares

Yield: 4 servings

4 oz cream cheese
2 Tbsp butter, softened
2 c cubed or slivered cooked chicken
¼ tsp salt
¼ tsp freshly ground black pepper
2-3 Tbsp milk
1-2 Tbsp chopped green onion
1 (4 oz.) can water chestnuts, coarsely chopped
1 (8oz) container refrigerator crescent rolls
¼ c crushed coupons
2 Tbsp butter, melted

Preheat oven to 350 degree. Blend cream cheese and butter until smooth. Add chicken salt, pepper, milk, onion and water chestnuts. Separate dough into 4 rectangles; firmly press perforations to seal. Divide chicken mixture evenly and place in center of each rectangle. Pull corners of each rectangle to center above chicken mixture, twist slightly. Pinch to seal-there may be small openings. Place on baking sheet. Brush tops of squares to 2 Tbsp melted butter, sprinkle with crushed croutons. Bake 20-25 minutes or until golden brown

Sally Baird

Appetizers & Beverages

Cocktail Meatballs

1 lb ground beef
1/3 c finely chopped onion
1 beaten egg
1 tsp salt
½ tsp worstershire sauce
½ c seasoned bread crumbs
¼ c milk
1 Tbsp minced parsley
1/8 tsp pepper

Combine above ingredients. Shape into bite size meatballs. Fry in skillet until browned on all sides. Drain fat. Add 1 bottle chili sauce and a 10 oz jar of grape jelly. Cover and simmer until warmed throughout. Serve with cocktail picks.
This is also great leftover served on white rice.

Linda Kidwell

Corn and Black Bean Tortilla Cakes

Serves 6

1 c rinsed & drained canned black beans, patted dry
1 ½ c fresh corn (2- 3 ears)
1 c finely chopped red onion
½ c finely chopped fresh cilantro
1 ½ c grated sharp white Cheddar (about 6 oz)
1 ½ c grated Monterey Jack (about 6 oz)
Twelve 6-to-7 inch flour tortillas
2 Tbsp olive oil
½ tsp cayenne or 1 tsp of chili powder
(for a smoky flavor, substitute 1 seeded & diced
canned chipotle pepper for cayenne or chili powder)
For garnish:
1 c sour cream
1 avocado, thinly sliced
Cilantro sprigs

In a bowl, toss together beans, corn, onion & cilantro. In another bowl toss together cheeses. Place 3 tortillas in one layer on a heavy baking sheet. Sprinkle each tortilla with 1/3 cup of bean mixture & 1/3 cup of cheese mixture & top with a second tortilla. Make two more layers on each tortilla in the same manner, gently pressing down each layer & ending with a fourth tortilla on top. (You may make up to this point 6 hours ahead, wrap tightly in plastic wrap, and chill.) Preheat oven to 450 degrees. In a small bowl, stir together olive oil and cayenne or chili powder. Brush over the top of each stack. Bake in the middle of oven 12-15 min until golden. Cut into wedges, garnish if desired with sour cream, avocado &/or cilantro sprigs.

Karen Pitkin

Cream Cheese Ball

1 (8 oz.) package cream cheese
½ bunch chopped green onions
1 ½ tsp Accent
½ tsp. Worstershire Sauce
1 pkg "Buddy" beef

Chop beef into small pieces. Retain ¼ of the packaged beef. Mix all remaining ingredients together. Roll into ball. Roll or pat remaining chopped beef on outside. Refrigerate at least 24 hrs prior to serving. Serve with your favorite crackers.

Linda Kidwell

Deviled Eggs

Boil 12 Eggs. Peel under cold running water, cut eggs in half lengthwise. Place cooked yolks in deep bowl. Mash with a fork until fine and crumbly. Add mayonnaise (or Miracle Whip) and mustard, a bit of ground pepper and a teaspoon of sugar. Mix all together until smooth and creamy. Spoon into eggs. Sprinkle with Paprika. Cover tightly and place in refrigerator until time to serve.

Hint: You can fill a cake decorator tube to fill the eggs and make them look professionally made. You can also add a slice of green or black olive, pimento, caviar, etc. to the top if you want to really make an impression!

Connie Rautenkranz

Easy Artichoke Dip

1 can Artichoke Hearts (not Marinated)
1 c Mayo
1 c Grated Parmesan Cheese

Chop artichokes, combine with mayo and parmesan cheese. Bake at 350 degrees for 30 minutes or until lightly golden brown. Serve with Melba Toast, crackers or chips.

*Note Mayo can be regular, light or fat free - do not substitute Miracle Whip

Carole Damon

Elegant Meat Balls

Preheat oven to 350 degrees
Makes about 40 one inch size meatballs

1 lb ground chuck
¼ c chopped yellow onion
1 finely diced clove of garlic
½ c fresh bread crumbs
½ tsp Tabasco sauce
2 Tbsp soy sauce
2 Tbsp milk
1 egg slightly beaten
½ tsp salt
½ tsp black pepper
1 tsp sugar

Combine all and form into small balls and bake for 15 minutes While meatballs are baking make the sauce (meatballs can be made the day before and refrigerated not baked, bake just prior to serving)

SAUCE:
2 c mayonnaise (do not use light or fat free)
4 Tbsp horseradish
1 tsp salt
4 Tbsp lemon juice
4 Tbsp dry mustard
½ lb sautéed till just tender small whole mushrooms

Combine all except meatballs and mushrooms in medium sauce pan till warm/hot DO NOT BOIL or sauce will curdle then add meatballs and mushrooms and stir till well coated with sauce.

Serve warm with slices of baguette if you have a chafing dish this works great

Jan Ryan

Fresh Salsa

3 lg ripe tomatoes, chopped
1 green bell pepper, chopped
1 red bell pepper, chopped
3 Serrano chile peppers, seeded and finely minced
1 firm but ripe avocado, cut into small cubes
½ c cilantro, chopped
½ medium red onion, chopped
1 clove garlic, pressed or finely minced
¾ tsp salt
½ tsp cumin
½ tsp lime zest
¼ c fresh lime juice

Combine all ingredients together. Chill for at least 1 hour.

Shannon Passwaiter

Fresh Salsa

3 medium tomatoes
1 small onion
1 or 2 jalapenos, depending on taste
3 cloves garlic
½ bunch cilantro
Juice of ½ lime
1 tsp salt

Place 1 tomato, 1/3 chopped onion, jalapenos, cilantro, salt & lime juice in food processor and puree. Dice remaining onion & tomato & add to mixture. Chill. Salsa is best if it sits for a few hours.

Becky Wann

Guacamole

3 lg. ripe avocados
Juice of 3 limes
1 hot red chili, chopped with the seeds
Salt
A handful of cilantro chopped.

Mash the avocados with a fork until pleasantly smooth but a little lumpy. Stir in salt, chili, and lime juice. Cover with plastic wrap pressing the plastic down onto the surface of the guacamole and refrigerate. When ready to serve taste for salt and lime and stir in the chopped cilantro

Candace Grover

Guacamole Dip

2-3 Avocadoes (ripe), pitted and peeled
1 pint Sour Cream
3-4 oz cream cheese
2 Tbsp Lemon juice
1 small to med. Onion, chopped
1-2 medium tomatoes, diced
1 3 oz. can black olives, chopped
1 lg. pkg shredded cheddar cheese

Smash avocados with a fork in medium to large bowl. Add sour cream and cream cheese, mix well. Add lemon juice. Fold in about 2/3 of the remaining ingredients. Place in a serving bowl and cover the top completely with remaining tomatoes, onions, black olives and cheese. Chill for about an hour before serving. Serve with tortilla chips.

Ruth Morton

Hot Artichoke Dip

Makes about 2 cups.

1 (16-oz) can marinated artichoke hearts (drained)
1/2 c Miracle Whip
1/2 c drained plain yogurt
1 c grated Parmesan cheese
Dash of paprika

Drain artichoke hearts and mash well. Add remaining ingredients, mix with fork and then sprinkle paprika on top. Bake at 350 for 30 minutes. Serve hot or cold. Good with pita points, Fritos Scoops or taco chips.

Rachel LaGrange

Hot Cocoa Mix

1 11oz. jar of Cremora
16 oz of Nestles Quick
1 pkg. (8 quarts) powdered milk
2/3 c of powdered Hershey's Cocoa
2 1/2 c of powdered sugar

Marilyn Kritzer

Hot Corn Dip

2 Tbsp. Unsalted butter
3 ½ c fresh white or yellow corn (can substitute with one pound bag of frozen sweet corn)
½ tsp salt
⅛ tsp freshly ground black pepper
1 c finely chopped yellow onion
½ c finely chopped red bell pepper
¼ c chopped green onion (green and white parts)
1 jalapeño, seeded and minced (optional)
2 tsp minced garlic
1 c mayonnaise
8 oz. shredded Monterey Jack cheese
¼ tsp cayenne pepper

Melt half the butter in skillet over medium-high heat. Add corn, salt and pepper. Cook about five minutes, stirring occasionally, until kernels turn deep golden brown. Pour into a mixing bowl.

Melt remaining butter in skillet. Add yellow onion and red pepper and cook about two minutes, stirring often, until onions are wilted. Add green onions, jalapeño and garlic; stir another two minutes. Pour mixture into bowl with corn and let cool.
Preheat oven to 350°.
Add mayonnaise, half the shredded cheese and the cayenne to the corn mixture and mix well. Pour into an eight-inch-square baking dish and sprinkle remaining cheese on top. Bake until bubbly and golden brown, 10 to 12 minutes.
Serve hot with tortilla chips.
Yields 6 cups dip; 12 to 18 servings

Fred Shick

Hot Crab Dip

Preheat oven 350-375 degrees
(Serves 6-8)

8 oz.   cream cheese softened to room temperature
1 Tbsp milk
1 Tbsp butter
2 Tbsp yellow onion chopped fine
1 medium leek chopped fine
8 oz.   crab meat
¼ tsp salt
¼ tsp black pepper
¼ tsp Worcestershire sauce
¼ tsp   Tabasco sauce (if you like a little "heat")
1-2 Tbsp dry sherry

Sauté onion and leek in butter just till light brown drain off butter
Mix with electric mixer all ingredients except crab fold in crab meat
Place in oven proof casserole. Bake 15-20 minutes. Serve assorted crackers
(I always double this and baking time will be 30/40 minutes)

Jan Ryan

Hot Ham & Cheese Spread

1 8 oz. pkg cream cheese
1 c shredded cheddar cheese
3 slices ham, diced finely

Mix all and put in small baking dish.
Bake at 350 degrees for 20 - 25 minutes or until lightly browned and puffed.
Serve with Ritz crackers or crackers of your choice.

Marnise Bounds Miller

Appetizers & Beverages

Hot Spinach Artichoke Dip

1 pkg. of frozen chopped spinach
1 can/jar artichokes
1 ½ c miracle whip
1 pkg. shredded mozzarella cheese
1 pkg. of Lipton vegetable soup mix or
2 ½ Tbsp of Ms. Dash no salt seasoning

Thaw and drain spinach. Drain and chop artichokes. Mix spinach, artichokes, mayo, seasoning & ½ cup of mozzarella cheese well. Place in oven safe dish and bake at 350 for 20 minutes. Top with extra mozzarella cheese & melt until lightly golden brown. Serve hot with tortilla chips, pita chips, torn bread or pita bread. Another great option is to mix in diced cooked chicken for a heartier appetizer. Enjoy!

Samantha Brummett

Italian Spritz

2 oz Prosecco
1 1/2 oz Campari
1/2 oz San Pelligrino Mineral Water
Slice of orange
1 Green olive

Fill an Old Fashioned glass with ice. Add Prosecco, Campari, & Mineral Water. Stir to combine, garnish with orange slice and olive on cocktail skewer.
Serves one (1)

Mary Gajewski

Jessica's Spin Dip

1 8 oz package of cream cheese
1 14 oz can of artichoke hearts (non-marinated works best)
½ c fresh spinach
¼ c mayonnaise (Hellmann's -- NOT Miracle Whip)
¼ c parmesan cheese
¼ c Romano cheese
1 garlic clove, minced
1 Tbsp of fresh Basil
Fresh mozzarella cheese
¼ tsp of sea salt
Salt and Pepper to taste

Mix together cream cheese, parmesan cheese, Romano cheese, garlic, basil, and sea salt by hand. Coarsely chop artichoke hearts and add to mixture along with spinach. Bake at 350 degrees.

I think that fresh ingredients work best for this dip, but the recipe is still great with dried spices and packaged cheese, etc.

Jessica Reed

Little Smokie Stogies

1 pkg little smokies sausages
1 lg pack corn tortillas
1 box toothpicks and hot oil

Two different sauces:
(1) ½ c mayonnaise plus 2 Tbsp yellow mustard
(2) ½ c mayonnaise plus 3 Tbsp ketchup

In hot oil, take tortilla and just soften it in hot oil, do not fry. Place on paper towel to drain. Put tortillas in stack and cut in 3 strips to roll sausage in. Then place each smokie on a strip and roll, use toothpick to hold in place. When all is rolled, heat oil to 350 degrees. Fry rolled smokies until tortilla is crisp. Let drain on paper towel and then serve with 2 sauces. Remove the toothpicks.

Darlene Cook

Orange Julius

6 oz orange juice
1 c milk
1 c water
1/4 to 1/2 tsp sugar
1 tsp vanilla
1 tsp almond extract
8 ice cubes

Mix thoroughly in blender

Linda Kidwell

Provolone Terrine Recipe

Ingredients

1/2 cup or 1 jar of sun dried tomatoes packed in oil (drain well & dice)
1 lb. deli sliced THIN provolone cheese
1 1/2 cup fresh basil (one plastic box of it in the produce section or one good bunch will get enough. You will only use the leaves so choose big leaves if possible)
1 cup parmesan cheese shredded (I have used the kind you put on pizza too if needed)
1/2 c olive oil
2 1/2 cloves of garlic (I use 3-5)
8oz. cream cheese (softened before mixes and spreads easier)
1/4 c butter
1/8 tsp pepper
1/4 cup pistachios (I use 1/2 cup or so. I buy the ones shelled already.) Crackers, bagel chips &/or baguette slices Cheesecloth (buy at Wal-Mart or in the kitchen dept. of some grocery stores-looks like gauze)
4x8 loaf pan

Pesto Prep

Combine basil leaves, parmesan cheese, olive oil and 2 cloves of minced garlic into food processor. Mix until well blended. Set off to side in separate bowl. I have used a basil pesto blend out of a jar and liked it. But the taste is better to me if fresh.

Garlic Cream Prep

Combine soft cream cheese, butter, 1/2 clove of garlic, peeper, pistachios into food processor. You may have to mix and remove some if your processor isn't big enough. Set to the side.

Terrine Prep

Cut cheesecloth to fit inside loaf pan and drape excess over edges enough to tie ends together. Wet cloth and wring dry before placing in loaf pan. (continued)

Appetizers & Beverages |23|

Cover bottom of pan with slightly overlapping slices of cheese and also about 2.5 inches up the sides. My pan fits 3 down each side and 1 on each end nicely. This will be the top of the loaf eventually. Divide the remaining slices in 3 equal stacks.

Layer as follows:

1/2 pesto
1 stack of provolone cheese (Spread out like you layered the bottom initially. You want it up the sides a bit so the next layer doesn't leak out)
1/2 sun dried tomatoes
all of garlic cream
remaining tomatoes
1 stack of cheese
remaining pesto
last stack of cheese

Fold cheesecloth over loaf and tie ends to help mold the shape. Chill at least 2 hours, but overnight is better- set out 1 hour before serving to soften. To serve, untie cheesecloth and invert pan on to a serving dish.
Garnish with basil/nuts if needed. Serve with choice of crackers.
Can chill up to 5 days.

Alice French

Rosemary Party Nuts

Makes about 6 cups

½ c unsalted cashews
½ c unsalted pecans (shelled)
½ c unsalted walnuts (shelled)
½ c unsalted hazelnuts
7 Tbsp fresh rosemary leaves
2 tsp. cayenne
2 Tbsp brown sugar
2 Tbsp coarse sale
3 Tbsp butter melted

Place nuts into a large baking pan. Toast in preheated 350° oven for about 10 minutes. Remove from oven. Toss with remaining ingredients.

Sarah Manis

Rye Babies

1 lb. Ground beef
1 lb. Sage pork sausage
1 lb. Velveeta
1 tsp. Garlic salt
1 tsp. Oregano
1 tsp. Red pepper flakes
2 loaves mini rye

Brown meats and drain, cut cheese into cubes and melt with meat and spices on low heat. Spread mixture of slices on rye. Broil on cookie sheet in oven until bubbly.

Faye Jameson

Sausage Balls

3 c Original Bisquick® Mix
1 lb bulk pork sausage
4 c shredded Cheddar Cheese (16 oz)
½ c milk

Heat oven to 350°. Lightly grease bottom and sides of 9X13 baking dish. Stir ingredients together with spoon or hands. Shape into 1 inch balls and place in pan. Bake 20-25 minutes or until brown. Immediately remove from pan.

Shauna Williams

Seven Layer Dip

Layer in order the following on a large platter with spoon:

1 can Refried Beans
16 oz. guacamole dip
16 oz. sour cream
1 lg. package shredded cheese (Mexican or Taco is good)
2 med. Tomatoes, chopped
½ c green onion
½ c chopped black olives (if desired)

Serve with tortilla chips
This is always a favorite at parties!

Ruth Morton

Simple Tofu Bites

16 oz. firm tofu
2 Tbsp soy sauce
1/2 tsp dried basil or Mrs. Dash seasoning

Preheat oven to 425 degrees. Slice tofu into small chunks (or slices if you want to serve as sandwiches). Marinate in soy & dried basil for at least two hours. Place tofu on greased non-stick pan and bake for 30 minutes. Tofu should become slightly browned.

Serve chunks on a platter with toothpicks as an appetizer. Serve slices in sandwiches. We are not vegetarians, but my kids really love this! They think tofu is a kind of cheese.

Susan Siena

Spiced Pork Meatballs with Guacamole

2 ½ lbs. ground pork
Salt
1 hot red chili pepper or several Thai or Bird Chilies chopped with seeds
1 Tbsp. chopped flat leaf parsley
1 Tbsp. chopped cilantro
1 tsp. fresh thyme
1 Tbsp. Dijon mustard
Zest of 1 lemon, grated.

Throw everything in a bowl and mix well, mix well with your hands and form into walnut sized balls. (the peppers can make your hands tingle, be careful not to touch your eyes after mixing) If you are going to refrigerate them to cook later, bring back to room temperature before frying. Fry in a dry pan until just crisped and no pink juices are flowing out of them. Arrange on a platter with guacamole for dipping. Meat balls should be warm when served.

Candace Grove

Spinach and Artichoke Dip

Makes 15-20 servings

¼ c butter or margarine divided
1 medium onion, diced
2 garlic cloves, minced
4 c fresh spinach, coarsely chopped
1 (4 oz) can artichoke hearts, drained and chopped
1 8oz package cream cheese, cut up
½ c mayonnaise
¾ c (3 oz) Parmesan cheese, shredded
1 (8 oz) 4-cheese country casserole blend shredded cheese
2/3 c pecans, chopped
½ herb seasoned stuffing mix

Melt 3 Tbsp of butter in large skillet. Add onion and garlic, sauté until tender. Add spinach and cook over medium heat, stirring for 3 minutes. Add artichoke hearts and the next four ingredients, stirring until cheese melts. Spoon into greased 2 qt. baking dish. Bake at 350° for 20 minutes, stir gently. Combine remaining 1 Tbsp butter, pecans and stuffing mix, tossing until blended. Sprinkle over top and bake 15 more minutes. Serve with Pita chips or French bread.

Sarah Manis

Spinach-Artichoke Dip

1 10oz pkg. frozen, chopped spinach
2 cans artichoke hearts, drained & chopped
½ c lite mayo
½ c fat free sour cream
1 ½ c grated Parmesan cheese
1 c shredded cheese, a white cheese is best

Preheat oven to 350°. Grease a 2-quart casserole dish. Squeeze water out of spinach. Combine all ingredients in a large bowl. Mix well. Place mixture in the prepared casserole dish and bake for 30 minutes.

Serve with bagel chips, tortilla chips, or toasted French baguette slices.

Tanalee Chapman

Spinach & Sausage Stuffed Mushrooms

(Makes 8 – 10 Servings)

1 pkg (12 oz) Stouffer's frozen Spinach Soufflé, defrosted
2 Tbsp butter or margarine
3 Tbsp chopped onion
¾ c water
2 ½ c herb seasoned stuffing (not crouton style)
½ lb bulk Italian sausage, thoroughly cooked, drained, and crumbled
¼ c grated Parmesan cheese, plus additional for garnish
2 ½ to 3 lb whole mushrooms, stems removed

MELT butter in medium saucepan; add onion and cook until translucent. ADD water, heat to boiling. Remove pan from heat. Add herb seasoned stuffing; stir until moistened. Stir in Spinach Soufflé, cooked sausage, and ¼ cup Parmesan cheese; stir well. ARRANGE mushrooms on baking sheet; fill with spinach mixture, mounding slightly. Sprinkle with additional Parmesan cheese. BAKE in preheated 4000 F oven for 10 to 15 minutes or until cheese and mushrooms are lightly browned.

Linda Kidwell

Tex Mex Dip

2 - 16 oz cans refried beans
3 ripe avocados
½ tsp salt
¼ tsp pepper
½ c mayonnaise
1 c sour cream
1 pkg McCormick's taco seasoning mix
1 bunch green onions, chopped
3 medium tomatoes, chopped
2 small cans chopped or sliced olives (optional)
2 or 3 c shredded longhorn cheddar cheese

Mash avocado, lemon juice, salt and pepper. Set aside. In separate bowl mix mayo, sour cream, and taco mix. Set aside. In a 13x9 pan layer the following: refried beans, avocado mixture, sour cream mixture, green onions, tomatoes, olives, and then the cheese. Chill at least 1 hour. Serve with tortilla chips.

Shannon Passwaiter

Tortilla Roll-ups

Two 8-oz packages of cream cheese
8 oz of sour cream
juice of one lime
small can of chopped peeled green chilies
small can of chopped black olives
3-4 Tbsp salsa or picante sauce
2 green onions-chopped fine
8-10 tortillas

Allow the cream cheese to soften at room temperature

Blend the first seven ingredients, ensuring that the cream cheese is well mixed. Spread a portion of the filling onto a tortilla, and roll the tortilla tightly. Place the tortilla crease side down on cookie sheet. Continue with the remainder of the tortillas or until the filling is exhausted. Refrigerate the tortillas overnight (or until the cream cheese has hardened, as this makes the next step easier).
Slice each tortilla into 3/4 to 1" segments, and serve with salsa or picante sauce. For an extra touch, add ½ of a ripe avocado to the filling.

James Becker

Uncle John's Cajun Wings

2 c white vinegar
1 c water
1 ½ tsp. finely minced garlic
1/3 tsp. Cornstarch
1 c sugar
¼ tsp. Tabasco Sauce
1 tsp. Salt
2 tsp. Ground ginger
4 Tbsp. Karo Syrup
1 ½ tsp. Chili powder

Combine all ingredients in large kettle. Bring to boil. Carefully add chicken wings (about 2 pounds) to mixture. Return to boil. Lower heat and simmer about 15 minutes until chicken is done and sauce has formed a glaze on chicken. Serve warm. This is also great for chicken thighs if you want larger portions.
*Note: Boil outside or in well ventilated area as aroma can be a bit overpowering.

Linda Kidwell

Zucchini Fritters

1 lb zucchini (about 2 medium sized) coarsely grated
Kosher Salt
Ground Black Pepper
1 lg egg
2 scallions, finely chopped
½ c flour
½ c grape seed oil or olive oil
Sour Cream

Salt the zucchini with about 1 teaspoon of salt. Try to remove the excess moisture from the zucchini by squeezing it with paper towels. Let sit for 10 to 15 minutes. Whisk egg in a large bowl; add the zucchini, flour, scallions, and ¼ teaspoon of pepper. Mix to combine well. Heat oil in a large skillet over medium heat. Cook fritters in 2 batches. Drop six mounds of batter (2 tbsp each...NO MORE OR IT GETS SLOPPY) into the skillet. Flatten slightly. Cook, turning once, until browned, 4-6 minutes on each side.

Faye Jameson

Breads

Angel Biscuits

2 pkgs yeast
¼ c water
2 c buttermilk
¾ c shortening
4 c self rising flour

Dissolve yeast in water and set aside. Put the shortening and the flour in a bowl and cut the shortening in as you would for pie dough. Pour the buttermilk and yeast mixture in the bowl, blending well but not over beating. Gently roll out the dough on a lightly floured board and cut, using a biscuit cutter or a small glass. Put them on a greased pan and either refrigerate until ready to use or bake at 400 degrees for 10 to 15 minutes. If refrigerated, warm to room temperature before baking. May be frozen as well.

Marnise Bounds Miller

Apple Bread

½ c shortening
2 eggs
1 c sugar
1½ Tbsp milk
½ tsp vanilla
2 c flour
1 tsp baking soda
½ tsp salt
1 ½ c chopped apples
2 ½ Tbsp sugar
1 tsp cinnamon
1 tsp nutmeg

Cream together shortening, eggs and sugar. Beat in milk and vanilla. Sift together flour soda and salt and add to moist ingredients. Fold in apples. Combine remaining sugar, cinnamon and nutmeg in separate bowl. Grease bottom only of 9x5 loaf pan. Pour half the batter into pan, then half of the cinnamon sugar mixture, then add the remaining batter. Top with the remaining cinnamon sugar mixture. Bake at 350 degrees for about one hour. Toothpick inserted in middle should come out clean.

Shannon Passwaiter

Banana Sour Cream Coffee Cake

1 1/4 c sugar + 2 Tbsp divided
1/2 c chopped pecans
2 tsp ground cinnamon, divided
1/2 c butter or margarine, softened
2 large eggs
1 c mashed ripe banana (about 2 – 2 1/2 bananas)
1/2 c sour cream
1/2 tsp vanilla extract
2 c all-purpose flour
1 tsp baking powder
1 tsp baking soda
1/4 tsp salt

Stir together 1/4 cup sugar, pecans, and cinnamon; sprinkle half of mixture in a well-greased 12-cup Bundt pan. Set remaining mixture aside.
Beat butter at medium speed with an electric mixer until creamy; gradually add remaining 1 cup sugar, beating 5 to 7 minutes. Add eggs, 1 at a time, beating just until yellow disappears. Add banana, sour cream, and vanilla, beating at low speed just until blended. Combine flour and next 3 ingredients. Pour half of batter into prepared pan; sprinkle with remaining pecan mixture. Top with remaining batter and then sprinkle 2 Tablespoons of sugar and 1 teaspoon of cinnamon on top. Bake at 350° for 45 minutes or until a long wooden pick inserted in center comes out clean. Cool in pan on a wire rack 10 minutes; remove from pan, and cool on wire rack.
Yield 1 (10-inch) coffee cake

Amanda Chitwood

Corn Cake

2 boxes Jiff cornbread mix
2 cans creamed corn
½ c heaping white sugar
¾ c oil
2 eggs

Mix all ingredients and bake in greased 9 x 13 pan for 45 minutes at 350 degrees. This is very good with salsa and sour cream.

Shauna Williams

Cranberry Bread

2 c flour
1 c sugar
1 1/2 tsp baking powder
1 tsp salt
1/2 tsp soda
1/4 c butter
1 egg, beaten
1 tsp grated orange peel
3/4 c orange juice
1 1/2 c raisins
1 1/2 c cranberries, chopped

Sift dry ingredients. Cut in butter until mixture is crumbly; add eggs, orange peel and juice all at once. Stir just until mixture is evenly moist. Fold in raisins and cranberries. Spoon into 9x5x3 loaf pan.

Bake at 350 degrees for about 70 minutes. Remove from pan and cool on rack. Makes a great Thanksgiving bread.

Marnise Bounds Miller

Fabulous French Toast Casserole

1 Lg loaf of French bread (cubed)
13 eggs
½ c maple syrup
1 tsp vanilla
1 c milk
1 tsp salt
1 Tbsp cinnamon
8 oz cream cheese (cubed)
3 Tbsp powdered sugar

Layer half of bread in the bottom of a 13x9 greased baking pan. Place cubed cream cheese evenly on bread layer; place remaining bread cubes in pan.
Mix by hand eggs, milk, syrup, cinnamon, vanilla & salt then pour evenly over the bread making sure all the bread is coated. Place covered in refrigerator overnight. Preheat oven 350 degrees for 45 min. Cook for 30 min. covered with foil, remove foil for last 15 min. Sprinkle with powdered sugar. Serve with syrup, fruit, nuts or whip cream.

Pat Figg

Fantastic Pecan Rolls

24 frozen Rhodes white dinner rolls
1 c chopped pecans
1 c brown sugar
1 small box instant butterscotch pudding
1 stick melted margarine
Cinnamon to taste

Grease a 9x13 pan well (consider using Pam). Sprinkle pecans pieces on bottom of pan. Place frozen dinner rolls on nuts. Sprinkle brown sugar over rolls. Sprinkle pudding mix over rolls. Sprinkle on cinnamon to taste. Drizzle margarine overtop. Cover with saran wrap and leave out overnight in a cool place, such as a basement. Bake at 375 degrees for 20 minutes. Invert onto plate. *Rhodes white dinner rolls are found in the freezer section of the grocery store.

Patt Spahn

Grandma J's B-Bread

½ c   butter or margarine (room temp)
1 c   sugar
2   eggs
2   lg ripe mashed bananas
1½ c flour
1 tsp baking soda
¼ tsp salt
1 tsp vanilla
½ c   quick oats
¾ c   chopped nuts

Preheat oven to 350 degrees. Cream butter and sugar well. Add eggs. Add Bananas and mix well. Add flour, baking soda, salt and quick oats. Stir in nuts and vanilla. Bake in 5 X 9 greased bread pan or 2 smaller greased pans (what I use) for 50-55 minutes. Time may vary depending on pans. Faye Jameson

Faye Jameson

Joan's Delish Apple Bread

2 c flour
1 tsp baking soda
1 tsp baking powder
½ tsp salt
1/8 tsp ginger
1 tsp cinnamon
½ c butter or margarine
1 c sugar
2 eggs, beaten
½ c chopped nuts
2 c chopped apples
1 tsp vanilla

Preheat oven to 350 degrees. Set aside the first six ingredients mixed together. Cream butter, sugar and eggs. Add apples, nuts and vanilla. Stir into flour mixture. Pour batter into two greased pans (7.5" X 3.75") Sprinkle top with the following ¼ c sugar 1 ½ tsp cinnamon. Bake at 350 degrees for 1 hour.

Faye Jameson

Monkey Bread

3 packages of buttermilk biscuit tubes
1 c sugar
2 tsp cinnamon
1 c butter
1/2 c packed brown sugar

Cut each biscuit into 4 pieces. Combine sugar and cinnamon. Roll each biscuit quarter in the sugar/cinnamon mixture. Drop the coated pieces into a well buttered Bundt pan. Do not squish the pieces together. Put 1/2 cup of the left over sugar/cinnamon mix, the brown sugar and butter into a small saucepan. Bring this mixture just to a boil; remove immediately from the heat. Carefully drizzle over the biscuit pieces. Bake at 350 for 30 minutes. Cool slightly in an upright position, then tip pan over onto a plate to remove the monkey bread. You're supposed to pull it apart to eat. Also, I sprinkle chopped pecans in as I am dropping the biscuit pieces into the Bundt pan.

Deb Tomaro

One Egg Banana Nut Bread

3 large bananas, mashed well
1 egg
1 stick butter, melted
1 ½ c Flour
1 c Sugar
1 tsp Salt
1 tsp Baking Soda
1 c nuts (I've used pecans & walnuts)

Mix all ingredients in a mixing bowl; put into a well greased loaf pan. Bake at 350 degrees for about 60 minutes, or until a knife inserted in middle comes out clean.

Laryn Pfrommer

Pumpkin Bread

3 c sugar
1 c coconut oil
4 eggs
2 c pumpkin
2/3 c water
3 1/2 c flour
2 tsp baking soda
1 1/2 tsp salt
3 tsp pumpkin pie spice (or 2 tsp cinnamon + 1 tsp nutmeg)
Add chocolate chips to liking

First, mix sugar & shortening together in large bowl, then add eggs, water, & pumpkin. Next, add spices, baking soda, salt, and flour. Then stir the chocolate chips into mixed batter. Grease 4 bread pans and bake at 350 for 45 minutes to 1 hour.
Sometimes I do half coconut oil and canola oil

Sally Baird

Pumpkin Bread

Sift together:
3 1/2 c flour
2 tsp   salt
2 tsp   cinnamon
2 tsp   nutmeg
2 tsp   baking soda

In a separate bowl mix together:
4   eggs
3 c   sugar
3/4 c water
1 tsp vanilla
1 c   cooking oil
1 c   nuts (if desired)
2 c   pumpkin

Add floured ingredients with moist ingredients. Place in greased & floured pans and bake for 1 hr (or until a toothpick comes out clean) @ 350. Makes 2 loaves.

Marilyn Kritzer

Pumpkin Bread

3 c sugar
2 c canned pumpkin
4 eggs
3 ½ c flour
1 ½ tsp salt
1 tsp cinnamon
1 c vegetable oil
2 tsp baking soda
2/3 c water
¼ c finely chopped nuts (optional)

Preheat oven to 350 degrees. Mix all ingredients in large bowl and pour into ungreased loaf pans. Bake for approximately 1 hour. Check for doneness by inserting toothpick in center. Check at 50 minutes. Let cool before removing from pans. Makes 3 loaves

Linda Kidwell

Rise & Shine Biscuits

1/3 c sour cream
1/3 c club soda
2 tsp sugar
2 c Bisquick

Mix and shape into balls or flatten out and cut with glass. Bake in greased pie pan at 425 degrees for 15 minutes.
Makes 6 biscuits.

Marnise Bounds Miller

Warm Stuffed Cheesy Bread

1 large French bread
2 pkg cream cheese
1 16oz tub sour cream
1 small can green chilies
1 pkg mild cheddar cheese

Cut out center of the French loaf (making it look like a boat). Set aside In a large bowl, mix all the ingredients together until it is blended really well. Place the French loaf on foil and a baking sheet. Put mixture in the center of the French loaf until it is full. Cover with foil. Bake at 350 degrees for 45 min. Serve warm. Use the center piece that was cut out to dip the warm cheesy mixture. Cut and eat.

Sherry Susnick

Zucchini Bread

Sift Together:
3 c flour
1 tsp baking powder
1 tsp baking soda
1 tsp salt
1 tsp cinnamon
Blend Together:
3 eggs
3 c sugar
2 c zucchini (make pulp in blender)
1 c cooking oil
2 tsp vanilla

Mix dry ingredients with moist ingredients and add 1/2 cup of nuts (if desired). Bake @ 350 for about 1 hour or until an inserted toothpick comes out clean. Makes 2 loaves.

Marilyn Kritzer

Casseroles, Veggies, & Sides

Aunt Ginny's Delight

16 slices sandwich bread – remove crust
8 slices Old English cheese (or American Deluxe)
½ lb shaved ham
7 eggs
1 tsp salt
3 c milk
1 ½ tsp dry mustard
3 c corn flakes
¼ lb butter melted

Mix eggs, salt, milk and dry mustard in bowl. Then layer in 9X13 ungreased pan 8 slices of bread, then ham and cheese, then remaining 8 slices of bread. Top with egg mixture. Crush corn flakes and put on top. Melt butter and drizzle on top. Cover with foil and let stand in refrigerator overnight. Bake for 1 hour at 300°.

Gary Paine

Baked Beans

2 – 16 oz cans pork & beans, drained
1 medium apple – peeled, cored, and chopped
1 medium onion – chopped
1/3 c ketchup
3 Tbsp brown sugar
3 Tbsp Worcestershire
2 Tbsp horseradish

Combine all ingredients. Bake at 325 degrees for 1 ½ to 1 ¾ hours

Linda Kidwell

Breakfast Casserole

1 lb sausage
6 slices bread, cubed
6 eggs
1 cup cheddar cheese, shredded
1 tsp dry mustard
2 cups milk

Preheat oven to 350 degrees. Brown sausage in skillet, drain grease. Mix all ingredients together and place in a 9x13 pan. Cover and refrigerate overnight. Bake for one hour.

Jill Smith

Broccoli Casserole

1 family size bag of chopped broccoli
1 sleeve Townhouse or Ritz crackers
1 stick of butter melted
1-2 oz block of cream cheese softened

Cook broccoli. Drain and put in 9X13 baking dish. Cover broccoli with softened cream cheese. Melt butter and add crushed up sleeve of crackers. Cover top of cream cheese and broccoli. Bake at 350 degrees until crackers are brown.

Shauna Williams

Corn Casserole

1 can whole kernel corn, partially drained
1 can cream style corn
8 oz sour cream
1 box jiffy corn muffin mix
1 stick butter
2 eggs, beaten
1 Tbsp sugar

Preheat oven to 400 degrees. Melt butter, mix with whole kernel corn, cream style corn, sour cream, corn muffin mix, eggs and sugar. Place in greased 9x13 pan. Bake for 40-50 minutes, or until browned.

Jill Smith

Cabbage & Rice Casserole

2 Tbsp bacon drippings
2 Tbsp butter or oil
3 c finely shredded cabbage
1 small onion, chopped
1 c Minute Rice, uncooked
2 c chopped tomatoes
salt & pepper to taste
1 green pepper, chopped (optional)
5 slices bacon, fried crisp and crumbled

Melt drippings and butter (or oil). Stir in cabbage, onion, pepper. Simmer, covered, about 10 minutes. Fold in remaining ingredients except bacon. Heat well. Add crumbled bacon.

Marnise Bounds Miller

Cheesy Chicken Nugget Casserole

1 pkg (71/4 ounces) macaroni & cheese dinner
1 pkg (10 ounces) frozen broccoli cuts, thawed
1 pkg (10 ounces) chicken nuggets

Prepare macaroni and cheese as directed on package. Add to 2-quart casserole with broccoli and mix; top with nuggets. Bake at 350 degrees, 30 – 35 minutes. Makes 6 servings

Lori A. Porter

Cheesy Potato Casserole

Ingredients:
¼ c butter, melted
1 small onion, diced
2 lbs frozen hash browns, thawed
1 can cream of mushroom soup
12-16 oz shredded cheddar cheese
1 pint of sour cream

Combine all ingredients in a large mixing bowl and mix well. Spread into a 9x13 pan that has been sprayed with cooking spray. Bake at 350° for 1 ½ to 2 hours until golden brown. This recipe is always a big hit at pitch-ins and is very easy to make. It can be prepared the night before, placed in the refrigerator overnight, and simply bake it in the morning.

Alan Pemberton

Cheesy Taco Bake

1 lb ground beef
1 pkg. taco seasoning
½ c water
1 can whole kernel corn, drained
1-8oz can tomato sauce
1 pkg jiffy corn muffin mix
1 egg
1/3 c milk
8 oz cheddar cheese, shredded

Preheat oven to 400 degrees. Brown ground beef and drain grease. Stir in taco seasoning, water, corn and tomato sauce; cook together until mixed. Add cheese; remove mixture from heat when melted. Pour mixture into 2 qt. casserole. In a separate bowl, prepare corn muffin mix according to package directions with egg and milk. Spoon corn muffin mixture over top of casserole. Bake, uncovered for 20-25 min.

Jill Smith

Chicken Casserole

1 box Stove Top Stuffing
1 c sour cream
1 can cream of chicken soup
4 Tbsp butter or margarine
3 to 4 chicken breasts, boiled and cut in small pieces
Broth from chicken

Melt butter in 9 x 13 baking pan. Pour 1/2 of the stuffing over butter. Place chicken on top of stuffing. In bowl, mix soup, sour cream and 1 cup chicken broth together. Pour over chicken. Top with remaining stuffing. Pour 2/3 cup broth over top. Bake at 350 degrees until slightly browned and bubbly.

Marnise Bounds Miller

Corn Pudding

2 c corn (canned or taken off cob)
4 Tbsp flour
1 Tbsp butter or margarine
2 tsp sugar
2 eggs (well-beaten)
2 c milk
Salt to taste

Mix corn, flour and sugar together. Combine eggs, melted butter and milk. Mix with corn mixture. Pour into greased baking dish. Bake at 350 degrees for 1 hour. Stir from the bottom 2 or 3 times during the first 30 minutes of baking time.
Serves 4

Barbara Joseph

Drunken Green Beans

1 lg can chopped green beans
4 strips chopped bacon
½ chopped onion
8 oz fresh mushrooms
1 Tbsp cognac

Sauté bacon and onion until bacon is crisp. Add Tbsp water if bacon begins to stick to pan. Add mushrooms. Sauté until mushrooms are tender. Add green beans and cognac. Cover and simmer about 15 to 20 minutes.

Linda Kidwell

Gourmet Baked Beans

1 pound ground beef
1 c chopped onion
2 16 oz cans butter beans, rinsed & drained
2/3 c packed brown sugar
½ c ketchup
4 Tbsp molasses
1 tsp chili power
10 strips bacon
4 16 oz cans pork & beans, un-drained
2 16 oz beans kidney beans, rinsed & drained
½ c bar-b-q sauce
4 Tbsp prepared yellow mustard
1 tsp salt

In saucepan over medium heat, brown ground beef, bacon & onion: drain. Add beans. Combine remaining ingredients; stir into bean mixture. Pour into a greased 5 quart baking dish. Bake uncovered at 350 degrees for one hour or until beans reach desired thickness. Serves 24 people.

Brenda Badger

Hash Brown Casserole

1 lb frozen hash browns
1 can cream of chicken or mushroom soup (undiluted)
½ c chopped celery
½ c chopped onion
1 c sour cream or plain yogurt
¼ stick butter or margarine
1 tsp salt
½ c grated cheddar cheese

Allow the potatoes to thaw enough to mix with other ingredients. Add other ingredients and mix together in large bowl. Pour into greased casserole dish. Bake for 1 hour at 350 degrees. Sprinkle with crumbs or french fried onions for the last 15 -20 minutes of baking time.

Barbara Joseph

Hearty Breakfast Custard Casserole

1 lb (2 medium to large) baking potatoes
Salt & Pepper
8 oz bulk low-fat sausage, cooked and crumbled, or 6 ounces finely chopped diced ham, or 6 oz turkey bacon, cooked and crumbled
1/3 c julienne-sliced roasted red pepper or 2 ounce jar sliced pimentos
3 eggs
1 c low-fat milk
3 Tbsp chopped chives or green onion tops
Salsa and low fat yogurt (optional)

Heat oven to 375 degrees. Butter 8 or 9 inch square baking dish or other small casserole. Peel potatoes and slice very thin; arrange half of potatoes in prepared baking dish. Sprinkle with salt and pepper. Cover with half of sausage or ham. Arrange remaining potatoes on top. Sprinkle with salt and peppers. Top with remaining sausage and red pepper. Beat eggs, milk and chives until blended. Pour over potatoes. Cover baking dish with aluminum foil and bake 35 to 45 minutes, or until potatoes are tender. Uncover and bake 5 to 10 minutes more. Serve with salsa and yogurt, if desired. Makes 4 to 5 servings.

Lori A. Porter

Porter's Slop

1 large round steak cut into 4 pieces
2 cans sliced potatoes
1 can cut carrots
1 jar spaghetti sauce

Brown the round steak in a large skillet. Turn the heat to simmer and add the canned potatoes and carrots and spaghetti sauce. Cover and let simmer until the sauce bubbles. Sprinkle shredded cheese or Parmesan cheese over the top if desired. Makes 3-4 servings.

Bob Porter

Sausage Casserole

1 lb sausage
1/2 c chopped onion
1 can cream of chicken soup
3/4 c uncooked rice
1/4 tsp salt
1 c celery, diced
1 c green pepper, chopped
1 1/2 c milk
1/2 tsp poultry seasoning

Brown sausage and drain. Add celery, onion, green pepper and soup. Simmer 15 minutes.
Mix rest of ingredients and add to sausage mixture. Pour into casserole dish and bake 50 minutes at 350 degrees. While casserole is baking, break 2 slices of bread into small pieces. Pour about 2 tablespoons melted butter on bread pieces to coat. Add bread on top of casserole the last 5 minutes of baking time.

Marnise Bounds Miller

Sautéed Green Beans

1 lb green beans, washed, trimmed and halved
4 bacon slices
1 16 oz bottle cocktail onions, drained
2 tsp sugar
¼ tsp thyme
1 Tbsp cider vinegar
¾ tsp salt
½ tsp black pepper

Cook green beans in boiling water until crisp tender. Drain thoroughly. In large skillet cook bacon until crispy. Remove bacon but leave drippings in pan. Crumble bacon and set aside. Cook onions, sugar, and thyme in drippings until golden brown. Add the green beans and cook until thoroughly heated. Add vinegar, salt, and pepper and toss to coat. Stir in bacon just before serving.

Shannon Passwaiter

Seafood Casserole

1 box Manicotti
Can of water packed tuna, drained (or use pouch)
1 lb cooked, shelled shrimp
1 can chopped clams, drained (or can use pouch)
8 oz fresh sliced mushrooms
1 Tbsp butter
1 Tbsp olive oil
1 lg jar alfredo sauce
1 lb grated mozzarella
3-4 Tbsp Italian seasoned bread crumbs

Cook manicotti according to directions. Sauté mushrooms in the butter & oil until tender. In a greased casserole dish, layer 1/2 the manicotti, tuna, shrimp, clams, mushrooms, and cheese. Top with 1/2 the alfredo sauce and mozzarella. Repeat for 2nd layer. Top with seasoned bread crumbs. Bake in 350 degree oven for 45 min.

Linda Kidwell

Turkey Tetrazzini Casserole

1/2 package egg noodles (cooked)
1 can cream of mushroom soup
1 stalk celery, diced
1 medium onion diced
Potato chips
1 1/2 cups cubed turkey

Combine all ingredients in casserole dish. Sprinkle top with crushed potato chips. Bake at 325 degrees for 45 min to an hour.

Linda Kidwell

Veggie Chili

The texture of the bulgur wheat is surprisingly like that of ground beef (but without fat & cholesterol). You won't taste the pumpkin that's added I promise! But, it does help make the chili smooth and creamy plus it adds lots of vitamin A.
Serves 6   30 minutes total time to make

5 ½ c water
¾ c bulgur wheat
2 tsp olive oil
1 c chopped onion
1 c chopped red pepper
2 Tbsp salt-free chili powder
2 tsp minced garlic
2 tsp ground cumin
1 can (28oz) crushed tomatoes
1 can (15oz) 100% pure pumpkin
1 medium zucchini, diced
1 c frozen corn
1 can (15.5 oz) low-sodium black beans, rinsed
½ c chopped cilantro
Garnish: reduced-fat sour cream & reduced-fat cheddar cheese

1. Put 3 cups of the water and the bulgur in a medium microwave-safe bowl. Cover and microwave on high until bulgur is tender, about 15 minutes.
2. Meanwhile, heat oil in a large soup pot and add onion and pepper and sauté 5 minutes. Add zucchini and sauté. Add chili powder, garlic and cumin; sauté until fragrant.
3. Add remaining 2 ½ cups water, the tomatoes, pumpkin, and corn; bring to boil over medium-high heat. Reduce heat and simmer 10 minutes, stirring occasionally, until vegetables are tender.
4. Stir in beans and bulgur; heat through. Remove from heat and garnish individual bowls with cilantro, sour cream and cheddar cheese

Andrea Reeves

Yuma Seta

2 lbs ground beef
1 onion
1 can tomato soup
1 can cream of chicken soup
1 tsp brown sugar
1 pkg noodles
Velveeta cheese

Brown 2 lb ground beef with 1 chopped onion. Drain. Then add 1 can tomato soup and 1 tsp brown sugar. Next cook 1 package noodles of your choice until almost done.

Drain and add 1 can cream of chicken soup. Mix well. Layer ground beef mixtures with noodle mixture in casserole dish. Add Velveeta cheese on top. Bake at 350 degrees until hot and cheese is melted.

Marnise Bounds Miller

Cookies & Candies

Brownies

2 sticks butter, melted
2 c sugar
2 tsp vanilla
¾ c cocoa
4 eggs
1 c flour
½ tsp baking powder
¼ tsp salt
1 c chopped nuts

Preheat oven to 375° Cream butter with sugar and beat until smooth. Add cocoa and vanilla and beat until smooth. Add eggs one at a time, beating after each addition. Sift dry ingredients together and add to egg mixture. Fold in chopped nuts.

Bake for 25-30 minutes.

Becky Wann

Chocolate Popcorn

What a simple, easy treat. Change the color of the chocolate to match the occasion. Red and green for Christmas, red for 4th of July, lavender and yellow for Easter, orange and brown for Thanksgiving and any color that matches a wedding or shower colors.

Pop what ever amount of popcorn you want for the event. Put clean newspaper down on a flat service and then foil over the news paper and spread the popcorn in one level as close together as possible. Then melt chocolate in microwave, do 30 seconds at a time, stir with a fork, and when melted take the for, and fling it over the popcorn covering in a splattered way until there is a good covering, let dry and then turn and sprinkle on the other side. When dry store in tight container until ready to serve. Will keep a week.

Gretchen Scott

Easy Mint Delights

2 egg whites
2/3 c sugar
2 or 3 drops green food color
¼ tsp. mint flavor
6 oz chocolate chips

Whip egg whites and fold in remaining items. Heat oven on to 400°, while you drop spoonfuls of the batter onto wax paper covered cookie trays. When oven reaches 400°, TURN OFF OVEN, and set cookie trays in oven for cookies to set. Can be left overnight in oven to set.

Sandy Sabbagh

Gooey Brownies

½ c unsweetened cocoa
1 c Crisco oil
2 c sugar
4 eggs
1 c flour
2 tsp vanilla
1 tsp salt

Mix cocoa, sugar & oil. Beat eggs and add cocoa mixture. Add other ingredients in order. Pour into greased 13 x 9 pan. Bake at 325 degrees for 30-40 minutes.

Brenda Badger

Mississippi Mud

2 c sugar
2 sticks margarine
4 eggs, beaten
½ c cocoa
1 ½ c flour
1 1/2 tsp baking powder
1 c chopped pecans
pinch of salt
1 bag marshmallows

Frosting:
1 box 10X powdered sugar
½ c canned milk
1/3 c cocoa
1 stick margarine
1 tsp vanilla

Make frosting, set aside. Cream sugar and margarine. Add beaten eggs. Add cocoa, flour, baking powder and salt. Stir in pecans. Spoon into 13"x9" greased and cocoa coated baking pan. Bake at 350 degrees for 30 minutes. While hot, pour 1 small bag of marshmallows on top of cake and let melt. Spread frosting on cake while still warm.

Frosting: Cream margarine; add sugar and other ingredients. Spread on cake.

Darlene Cook

My Mom's Brazil Nut Sticks

2 c ground Brazil Nut Meats
2 eggs
2 c brown sugar
2 c flour
½ tsp salt
1 tsp vanilla
½ tsp baking powder

Mix all ingredients well in order given. If dough does not mold easily add more egg. Roll in stick shape about 1 ½ inch long, ½ inch round Bake on greased cookie sheets at 350° for 10-12 minutes. Cool on wire racks.

Sandy Sabbagh

No-bake Chocolate Oatmeal Cookies

2 heaping tablespoons cocoa
1 c sugar
1 stick butter or margarine
2 heaping tablespoons peanut butter
½ c milk

Heat until mixture comes to a rapid boil. Boil 2 minutes. Remove from heat. Immediately add ½ tsp vanilla, 3 c oats. Mix well and drop by tablespoons onto wax paper.

Marnise Bounds Miller

Oatmeal Cookies

1 c butter flavored Crisco
1 c brown sugar
1 c granulated sugar
2 c flour
1 tsp baking powder
1 tsp salt
1 tsp soda
1 tsp vanilla
2 eggs, beaten
2 c quick oats
2 c chopped pecans

Cream Crisco and sugar add eggs and mix, add vanilla. Add sifted dry ingredients, Add oats and nuts. Bake @ 350° for 12 minutes.

Bonnie Skogland

Old Fashioned Sugar Cookies

1 c powdered sugar
1 c granulated sugar
1 c shortening
1 c butter
2 eggs, beaten
4 c flour
¾ tsp vanilla (I use light vanilla instead of dark to keep the dough white)
¾ tsp salt
¾ tsp tartar
¾ tsp soda

Cream shortening, butter, and sugars. Add eggs and mix well. Add remaining ingredients and stir. Form dough into oblong roll and chill. Slice thin. Bake at 350 degrees for 6 to 8 minutes. Dough can also be rolled out and cut into shapes. Colored sugar can be applied before baking.

Laryn Pfommer

Peanut Butter Fingers

½ c butter
½ c cane sugar
½ c brown sugar
1 egg
1/3 c peanut butter
½ tsp baking soda
¼ tsp salt
½ tsp vanilla
1 c flour
1 cup rolled oats

Mix sugar and butter, add eggs, add peanut butter, stir in dry ingredients, add vanilla
Grease 9x13 baking pan, spread batter in pan.
Bake at 325 degrees for 15 to 20 minutes
While cookies are baking, make glaze:
2/3 c powdered sugar, 1/3 c peanut butter, and 2-4 Tbsp of milk
Glaze cookies while still slightly warm, cut into bars.

Carolyn Rogers Richard

Peanut Butter Fudge

No-Stick Cooking Spray
3 c sugar
½ c butter or margarine
2/3 c Evaporated Milk
1 2/3 c Jif Creamy Peanut Butter
1 (7 oz) jar marshmallow crème
1 tsp vanilla extract

Spray 13 x 9 x 2-inch pan with a not-stick cooking spray. Combine sugar, butter and milk in large saucepan, stirring constantly on medium heat, until mixture comes to a boil. Reduce heat and simmer 5 minutes, stirring constantly. Remove from heat. ADD peanut butter. Stir until well blended. Add marshmallow crème and vanilla. Beat until well blended. Spread in prepared pan. Cool.

Shauna Williams

Porcupine Cookies

These are a macaroon style cookie, with a chewy texture. Dried apricots can be substituted for the dates.

2 large eggs
¾ c sugar
2 c diced pitted dates
1 c chopped walnuts or pecans
Flaked coconut
(scant flour if desired)

Preheat oven to 300 degrees
In a large deep bowl, whisk eggs until slightly foamy. Add sugar and whisk until blended. Add dates and nuts. If desired, add ¼ cup flour (or less) so that "dough" is easier to handle. Dough will be thin. Drop rounded Tbsp of dough into flaked coconut and form into small ball. Place on a lightly greased cookie sheet and cook in slow oven until the coconut is well browned. These will keep for two weeks in an airtight container.

Karen Pitkin

Raspberry Danish Dessert

Crust:
2 c flour
½ c brown sugar
1 c nuts (if desired)
2 sticks butter

Filing:
16 oz softened cream cheese
2 c powdered sugar
1 tsp vanilla
1 tub of whipped topping (large size)

Topping:
1 c water
1 c sugar (1/2 now and ½ later)
2 c frozen raspberries
3 Tbsp cornstarch
2 Tbsp raspberry gelatin

For crust: Melt butter and mix all ingredients together, Bake 10-15 minutes at 350° - do not over bake. When cool, crumble into pan, saving some for topping.

For filling: Soften cream cheese: mix in powdered sugar until creamy; add vanilla and whipped topping. Set aside.

For topping: In saucepan, mix all ingredients together. On medium heat, bring to full boil, stirring constantly to prevent scorching. Boil 1-2 minutes until mixture begins to thicken. Turn off heat and add remaining ½ cup sugar. Let cool; mixture will thicken.

Spread filling over crust. When topping cools, pour over cream cheese mixture and sprinkle remaining crust over topping. Cool in refrigerator.

Darlene Cook

Shortening Sugar Cookies

Cream 1 ½ c Sugar with 1 c Crisco. Add 3 eggs beating after each addition. Add 1 tsp. vanilla, ½ tsp. pure almond extract. Sprinkle 1tsp. baking soda, and ½ tsp. salt over mixture and mix, then add 4 ½ c flour. Mix flour in slowly.

Use flour and sugar on counter to roll and cut to desired shape for the season. Bake on cookie sheets at 350° for 8 to 10 minutes. Loosen immediately, cool and frost if desired.

Sandy Sabbagh

Snicker doodles

½ c butter
½ c Wesson oil
2 eggs
1 ½ c sugar
2 ¾ c flour
1 tsp baking soda
¼ tsp salt
2 tsp cream of tartar
4 Tbsp sugar
4 Tbsp cinnamon

Cream together butter and sugar, add in oil and eggs. Mix together all dry ingredients. Mix 4 Tbsp. of sugar and 4 Tbsp of cinnamon together in small bowl. Take 1 Tbsp of cookie dough, roll in ball, then roll in combined sugar mixture. Bake at 400° for 8-10 minutes.

Darlene Cook

Sugar Bars

¾ c flour
¾ tsp baking powder
¼ tsp salt
¼ c butter or margarine
1 c brown sugar
2 eggs
1 tsp vanilla
½ c chopped nuts (optional)

Grease and 8 x 8 or 9 x 9 pan. Beat eggs with butter. Add vanilla and brown sugar. Add combined dry ingredients. Bake at 350 degrees for 30 minutes. Cool and cut into bars.

Brenda Badger

Sweet-Heat Almonds

These sugar glazed hot-lipped little scorchers are amazingly addictive. Store them at room temperature, but keep them away from moisture and humidity, which can cause the glaze to soften. 4 servings

1 c whole almonds in their skins
¼ c sugar
¼ tsp cayenne

1. Heat a nonstick skillet over high heat for 1 minute. Add the almonds and reduce the heat to medium-low. Cook, stirring, until the almonds are lightly toasted, 3 to 4 minutes.
2. Add the sugar and keep stirring until the sugar melts and brown, about 30 seconds. (Be careful: Caramelized sugar can give a nasty burn) Immediately turn out the nuts onto a sheet pan and sprinkle with the cayenne and plenty of salt.
3. Wait for a minute or two, until the almonds are just cool enough to touch. Break them into individual almonds. Do not wait too long, or the sugar will harden and it will be difficult to separate the nuts.

Gretchen Scott

White Cookies

½ c sugar
½ c powdered sugar
1 egg
1 tsp vanilla
2 ¼ c flour
½ tsp cream of tartar
½ tsp baking soda
½ tsp salt

Sift together dry ingredients, set aside. Cream shortening, sugars and egg. Slowly mix in flour mixture. Chill 15 minutes. Roll dough into balls about the size of walnuts. Place on cookie sheets. Flatten with the bottom of a smooth glass that has been greased and dipped in sugar. Colorful sugar may be used. Try not to make them too thin. Bake at 350 degrees for 6-8 minutes.

Shannon Passwaiter

International Recipes

Baba Ganouj

1 ½ lbs eggplant
Juice of 1 lemon
2 Tbsp extra virgin olive oil
1 c strained, Greek style yogurt (Fage is a good brand)
2 – 3 crushed garlic cloves
Salt to taste
1 – 2 Tbsp chopped flat leaf parsley or fresh mint

Prick the eggplants all over and roast in a 475 degree oven, on a sheet of foil, for about 45 to 55 minutes, or until they feel very soft and the skins are wrinkled. When cool enough to handle, remove the skins, and place the eggplant pulp in a colander with small holes. Press out as much of the water as you can with your hands or a spatula. Place the pulp in a food processor and puree. Mix in the remaining ingredients and chill. Garnish with the parsley or mint and serve with fresh, warm pita pieces.

Candice Grover

Birouats

¾ lb ground lamb
¼ c minced onion
2 garlic cloves, minced
4 tsp ground cumin
1 tsp ground ginger
1 tsp paprika
¾ tsp ground cinnamon
Cayenne to taste
Large pinch of saffron threads, ground and soaked in a little warm water
2 Tbsp chopped fresh parsley
2 Tbsp chopped cilantro
Salt and freshly ground pepper to taste
1 egg lightly beaten (continue on next page)
½ lb phyllo
½ c melted unsalted butter

Combine lamb, onion, garlic, spices including saffron in water, cilantro, parsley and salt and pepper in a skillet and cook over medium heat, uncovered, stirring occasionally, until the lamb is cooked and the moisture has evaporated, about 6 minutes. Drain off and discard the fat. Add the egg and cook 1 more minute. Preheat oven to 375 F. Cut 3" width strips of phyllo. Brush one strip with melted butter and top with another strip and place a heaping teaspoon of the lamb on one end then fold over to form a triangle and fold up like a flag. Repeat making about 40 pastries. Place on a greased baking sheet and bake until golden brown, about 15 minutes. Serve warm or at room temperature.

Candy Grover

Cheesy Chicken Enchiladas

1 Tbsp vegetable oil
1/2 c chopped onion
1/8 tsp garlic salt
1-4 oz can green chilies
1 large can chicken - or cook 3 chicken breasts
1/4 c chicken broth
2 tsp chili powder
1 tsp cumin
4 oz cream cheese
6 flour tortillas
1/2 pound Velveeta cheese
2 Tbsp milk
1/2 c chopped tomato

Microwave onion and garlic salt in oil for 2 to 3 minutes. Stir in chicken, chilies, broth and seasonings and microwave 4 minutes. Add cream cheese and stir until melted. Put in tortillas and roll. Put in microwave safe baking dish. Microwave Velveeta and milk until cheese is melted. Mix well. Pour over tortillas. Microwave 6 to 8 minutes. Sprinkle chopped tomatoes on top.

Marnise Bounds Miller

Chicken Enchilada Ring

2 c coarsely chopped chicken
1/4 c chopped pitted ripe olives
1 c shredded Monterey Jack/Cheddar blend
1 can (4 oz.) chopped green chilies, undrained
1/2 c mayonnaise
1 Tbsp Southwestern Seasoning Mix
2 plum tomatoes
1 lime
2/3 c finely crushed tortilla chips, divided
2 pkgs crescent rolls
1 c salsa
1 c sour cream

Preheat oven to 375 degrees. Mix chopped chicken, olives, cheese, green chilies, mayonnaise and seasoning mix in bowl. Seed and chop one tomato. Slice lime in half. Juice one half of lime to measure 1 tsp of juice. Reserve remaining lime for garnish. Add chopped tomato and lime juice to chicken mixture. Reserve 2 Tbsp crushed chips and add remaining chips to chicken mixture. Mix well. Sprinkle reserved crushed chips over flat side of a large cutting board. Place dough onto chips and press down so chips adhere to dough. Separate dough into triangles. Arrange triangles, chip side down, in a circle on a 13" baking stone. Wide ends should overlap in the center and points should be toward the outside. There should be a 5" diameter opening in the center. Scoop chicken mixture onto the wide ends of the triangles. Bring points of the triangles up over filling and tuck under wide ends. Do not cover filling completely. It should show in between each triangle. Bake 20-25 minutes or until golden brown. For garnish, cut remaining tomato into 8 wedges. Cut remaining half of lime into 4 slices, cut in half. Arrange between openings of ring where filling is showing. Serve with salsa and sour cream.

Connie Rautenkranz

Chiles Rellenos

10 Anaheim Chiles
1 lb Monterey Jack Cheese, cut into 3"x 1" sticks (approx)
4 eggs separated
Flour
Salt
Cooking oil

Char the chilies over a gas flame or under a broiler turning to blacken all over. I cook mine on the grill during summer. Place blackened chilies in a bowl of water. Once cool enough to handle rub off skins. Cut off stem ends and pull out veins and seeds, you can rinse out the remaining seeds. Place the chilies on a large cutting board and stuff each with cheese. Sprinkle with a little salt then dredge in flour. Set aside. Beat 4 egg whites until foamy, add a pinch of salt, and then beat until stiff. Beat the 4 yolks in a separate bowl then fold into the whites. Working quickly dip chilies in eggs to coat. Fry chilies in 1" hot oil in a large skillet turning to brown evenly. These cook quickly. Drain on paper towels.

Shannon Passwaiter

Easy Beef Enchiladas

2 lb ground sirloin
1 pkg enchilada powder
1 can enchilada sauce
1 pkg burrito size soft taco shells
5 slices American cheese

Brown beef and drain. Add enchilada powder and ¼ cup water and simmer for 5 minutes. Fill taco shells with beef and roll. Once rolled place in 9X13 deep baking dish. Once the enchiladas are rolled add half a slice of American cheese on top of each enchilada and cover with enchilada sauce. Bake until cheese on top is melted. Great with shredded lettuce and sour cream.

Shauna Williams

Eggplant Parmesan

2 eggplants
Canola oil
lemon juice
7 eggs
1/2 c grated parmesan cheese
Italian seasoned bread crumbs
2 jars Ragu mushroom spaghetti sauce
1 pkg shredded mozzarella cheese

Cut off ends of eggplant. Peel. Slice eggplant into 1/2 inch slices. Put in canola oil and lightly salt each layer. Sprinkle each layer lightly with lemon juice. Beat eggs. Mix with 1/2 tsp salt, 1/2 tsp pepper, and grated parmesan. Dip each slice in egg mixture and then in seasoned bread crumbs. Fill frying pan 1/2 full of oil, or use deep fryer. Fry breaded slices in very hot oil until lightly browned on both sides. Drain on paper towels. After all are cooked, pour enough sauce to cover a roasting pan. Layer eggplant, sauce, and mozzarella. Repeat until all eggplant is used. Bake at 350 degrees for 1/2 hour. This also makes great sandwiches! Use garlic bread. Put under broiler or toaster oven until lightly browned. Add eggplant, top with grated cheese and put back in broiler until cheese is melted. Also makes a great side dish served over spaghetti.

Linda Kidwell

Hungarian Goulash

2 lb beef stew meat, 1" squares
1 large onion, sliced
1 clove garlic, minced
½ c catsup
2 Tbsp Worcestershire sauce
¼ c flour
1 Tbsp brown sugar
2 tsp salt
2 tsp paprika
½ tsp dry mustard
1 c water

Place meat in slow cooker pot; cover with sliced onion. Combine garlic, catsup, Worcestershire sauce, sugar, salt, paprika and dry mustard. Stir in water. Pour over meat. Cover and cook on low for 9 to 10 hours. Turn control to high. Dissolve flour in small amount of cold water and stir into meat mixture. Cook on high 10 to 15 minutes or until slightly thickened. Serve over noodles or rice. Serves 6

Brenda Badger

Italian Beef Stew

1 lb stew meat
3 carrots cut in 1" slices
2 potatoes, cubed
1/2 c diced celery
1 chopped onion
1 Tbsp plain tapioca granules
1 slice bread, cubed
1 small can stewed tomatoes, Italian style
1 tsp salt
1/2 tsp pepper,
1/2 tsp mixed Italian spice

Combine all ingredients in roasting pan or large casserole dish. Bake covered at 250 degrees for 5 hours.

Linda Kidwell

Lebanese Spinach and Rice

Brown about ¾ lb ground round with 1 chopped onion.
Pour off the fat and add:
3/4 tsp Cinnamon
¼ tsp Allspice
Salt and Pepper to taste
1 to 2 Tbsp flour to thicken slightly

Add 3/4 to 1 pound fresh spinach, washed, or 2 boxes frozen. Add a little water, about ½ cup. Simmer until spinach is done. Add lemon juice to taste (lemon juice should be noticeable) and mix in. Serve over hot rice. Serves 4 or 5 as main dish

Sandy Sabbagh

Muc Nhoi
(Vietnamese Stuffed Squid)

12 young whole squid, about 6" long, cleaned and skinned
½ lb ground pork
4 dried Shiitake mushrooms, soaked in hot water for 15 minutes, then stemmed and finely chopped
1 bundle cellophane noodles, soaked in hot water until soft and then cut into ¼ " lengths
½ small yellow onion, finely chopped
½ tsp minced fresh ginger
2 tsp fish sauce (3 Crabs brand is very good)
Freshly ground black pepper
¼ tsp sugar
¼ c canola or other neutral oil for frying

Remove the squid tentacles and finely chop and place in a bowl. Add the remaining ingredients and mix well. Pierce the tail end of each squid with a skewer. Using a pastry bag with a large plain pastry tip, fill each squid body loosely, about ¾'s full with the filling and stitch together the open end with a tooth pick. **Do Not Over Stuff.** As you stuff each squid place them on a paper towel to absorb any moisture possible. Heat the oil in a large skillet to medium high. Have a spatter screen handy. Lay each squid in the skillet and sauté about 2 minutes on each side. Then reduce the heat to low and continue to cook about 10 minutes until golden and firm. Remove and allow to cool. Then cut into about ¼" slices and arrange on a platter. Serve with Ginger Lime Dipping Sauce.

Candace Grover

Ginger Lime Dipping Sauce

1 2" piece of fresh ginger peeled and minced
5 Tbsp freshly squeezed lime juice
2 ½ tsp sugar
2-3 Tbsp fish sauce

Combine all and stir until the sugar is dissolved. Start with 2 Tbsp fish sauce and add the additional Tbsp if needed. Taste for sweet/sour balance and add either more sugar or lime juice as needed.

Candace Grover

Pollo en Mole Rojo Sencillo

1 large chicken (3 ½ - 4 pounds), cut in pieces
1 small white onion, coarsely chopped
2 cloves garlic, peeled and coarsely chopped
2 tsp salt
Water or light chicken broth to cover

Put all ingredients in a pan and simmer until chicken is nearly tender but not cooked through, about 25 – 30 minutes.

For the sauce:
2 oz chilies guajillos
2 oz chilies pasillas
2 oz chilies anchos
1/4 c oil
5 oz hulled raw pumpkin seeds
6-8 c chicken broth
3 whole cloves
4 garlic cloves, peeled and coarsely chopped
1 tsp salt

Remove stems and seeds from dried chilies. Put in a pan and cover with hot water, bring to a simmer and simmer for 5 minutes. Remove from the heat and allow to soak for 5 minutes. Drain and discard water. Heat half the oil in frying pan, add pumpkin sees and toss until they swell and pop. Watch carefully as they will burn easily. Put 1 c of broth in a blender, add spices and garlic and blend thoroughly. Put 1 c of broth and the seeds in the blender and blend until it forms a thick paste. Heat the rest of the oil in a frying pan, add the seed paste and fry over medium heat, stirring constantly and scraping the bottom of the pan to prevent burning. Add 2 c of broth and the chilies to the blender jar and blend half the chilies thoroughly. Add the remaining chilies and blend thoroughly. Add the chilies in broth and the spices in broth to the pumpkin seed mixture. Cook over medium heat for about 15 minutes. Add the remaining broth and cook an additional 15 minutes. Add the chicken pieces and cook for another 15 minutes. Sauce should be fairly thick.

Becky Wann

Pollo En Mole Verde
(Chicken in Green Mole)

1 large chicken (3 ½ - 4 pounds), cut in pieces
1 small white onion, coarsely chopped
2 cloves garlic, peeled and coarsely chopped
2 tsp salt
Water or light chicken broth to cover

Put all ingredients in a pan and simmer until chicken is nearly tender but not cooked through, about 25 – 20 minutes.

1 c raw sesame seeds
1/3 c raw hulled pumpkin seeds
3 whole cloves
3 whole peppercorns
3 whole allspice
2 ½ Tbsp oil
8 romaine leaves, coarsely chopped
½ bunch spinach, well washed and coarsely chopped
1 large bunch cilantro, washed and coarsely chopped
1 bunch flat leafed parsley, washed and coarsely chopped
2 large garlic cloves, peeled and coarsely chopped
2 large poblanos, seeds and veins removed, coarsely chopped
6 oz (about 8 medium) tomato verde or tomatillos

(continued)

International Recipes

Put the sesame seeds into an ungreased frying pan and heat over medium heat, stirring and turning over constantly, until they turn a dark golden color, about 7 minutes. Spread out on a large pan to cool. Add the pumpkin seeds to the pan and heat over medium heat, shaking the pan and stirring them until they start to swell up and pop, do not let them brown, about 3 minutes, cool. Fry the seeds in the oil for about 5 minutes, or until the seeds turn a rich, golden brown. Put 1 ½ cup chicken broth in a blender and add the romaine, spinach, parsley, garlic and poblanos. Add the tomatillos a small amount at a time. Add the pureed greens to the seed paste, stir well and cook over medium heat, stirring and scraping the pan frequently until the sauce begins to stick, about 15 minutes. Add the remaining broth and cook over medium heat until the sauce has reduced and thickened, about 15-20 minutes. Add the chicken pieces and cook for another 15 minutes. Sauce should be fairly thick.

Becky Wann

Shrimp Scampi

1 lb cleaned, deveined shrimp, tails on
1/2 stick butter
2 Tbsp extra virgin olive oil
8 - 10 whole cloves of garlic, peeled
1 pkg sliced mushrooms (optional)
Italian seasoned bread crumbs
Pecan rice (you can substitute angel hair pasta if you can't find the rice)

Prepare rice or pasta according to direction. In large skillet, combine butter & oil. Heat on medium low heat until foam is almost gone but not to the point where the butter begins to burn. Add garlic cloves and cook until golden brown over low heat. Remove garlic. Add shrimp. Sauté over low heat until shrimp are pink. Add bread crumbs to thicken sauce. Serve over the prepared rice or pasta. Great with some garlic bread and a salad.

Linda Kidwell

Tabhouleh (The Real Thing)
Lebanese Garden Wheat Salad

2 Bunches Parsley, with stems trimmed, chopped fine.
1 c Fresh Mint Leaves, chopped fine
2 Bunches green onion, chopped fine
4 Medium tomatoes, diced
¾ c bourghl wheat
Juice of 2 lemons

Mix the greens and tomatoes together. Set aside. Soak the wheat in a bowl covered with warm water. When the wheat is soft, squeeze it dry with hands, and mix it with the greens and tomatoes. The salad should be mostly green and red with the wheat
not conspicuous or gummy. Season with olive oil, salt, and lemon juice to taste to make a moist salad.

Sandy Sabbagh

Meat, Poultry, Fish

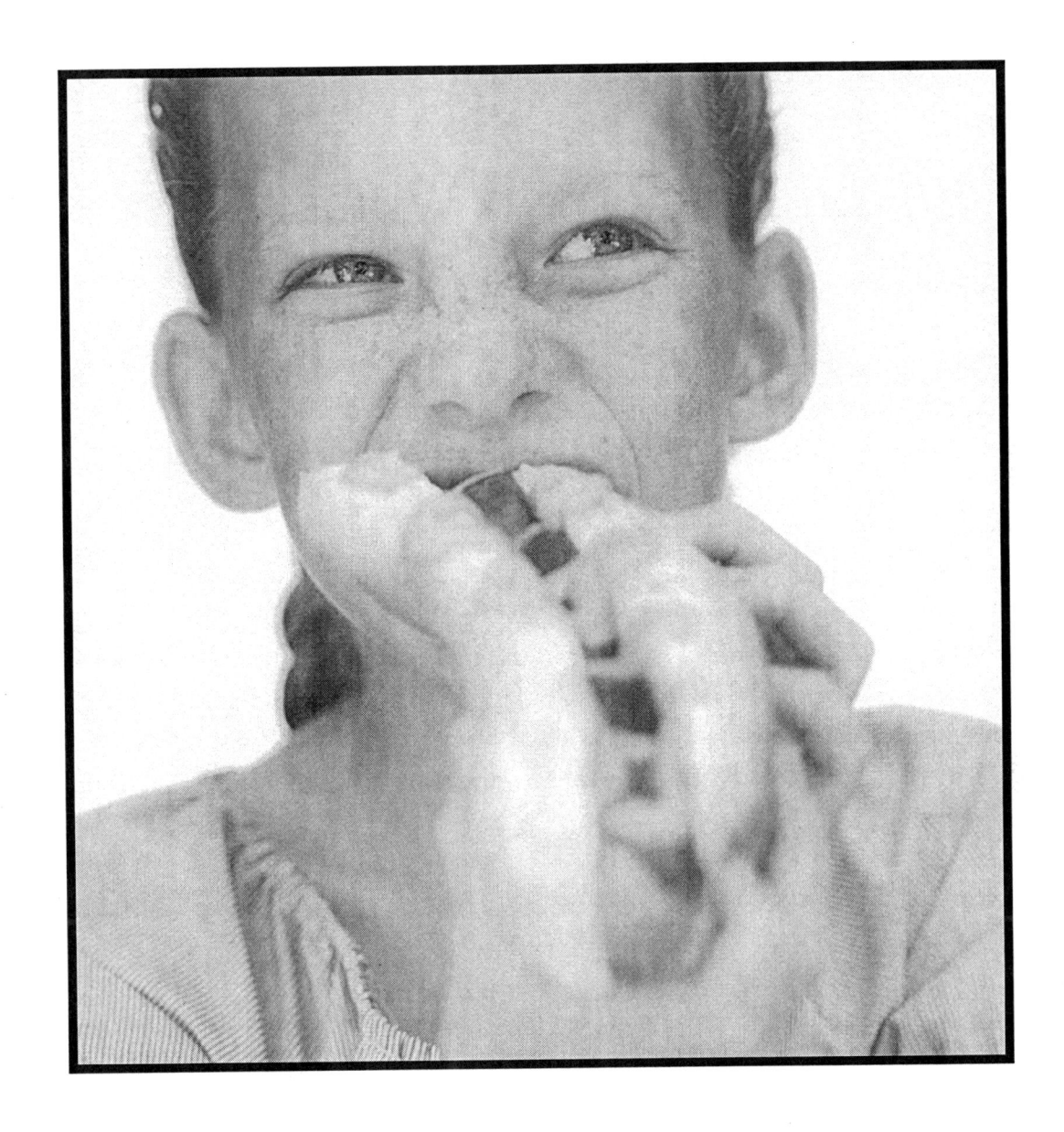

Baked Chicken in White Wine

1/2 c all purpose flour
1 tsp paprika
1/2 tsp of black pepper
1/2 tsp garlic powder
3 whole chicken breast (about 10 ounces each), split & skinned
1 1/2 c dry white wine
2 Tbsp margarine
2 Tbsp drained capers

Preheat oven to 450 degrees F. Combine flour with seasonings; dredge chicken in flour mixture. Arrange chicken breasts in baking dish and pour wine over. Dot with margarine and sprinkle with capers. Cover with foil. Bake 20 minutes, then reduce heat to 325 degrees F. and continue baking until chicken is cooked through, about 1 hour.

Beth Freeman

Chicken Cacciatore

In skillet, brown on a 2 ½ - 3 pound chicken breasts (I use boneless, skinless chicken breasts) in olive oil. Remove chicken. In same skillet, cook 2 medium Vidalia onions chopped or cut in ¼" slices, 2 cloves garlic minced until tender, but not brown, return chicken to skillet.

Combine:
1 lb can tomatoes
8 oz can tomato sauce
1 tsp salt
¼ tsp pepper
1 tsp dried oregano or basil, crushed
½ tsp celery seed
1-2 bay leaves

Pour mixture over chicken. Cover and simmer 30 minutes. Stir in ¼ cup dry wine. Cook chicken, uncovered, 15 minutes longer or until tender; turning chicken occasionally. Remove bay leaves, skim off excess fat. Ladle sauce over chicken in dish. Makes 4 servings.

NOTE:

I grill the chicken so there is no fat to drain or could bake it. I also simmer the complete dish for at least an hour or so before I add the dry white wine. As you know, the alcohol will completely evaporate so it won't hurt the children. Best if cooked a day before serving.

Gloria Yeary

Chicken Cordon Bleu

4 skinless, boneless chicken breasts
¼ tsp salt
1/8 tsp ground black pepper
6 slices Swiss cheese
4 slices cooked ham
½ cup seasoned bread crumbs

Preheat oven to 350. Coat a 7"x11" baking dish with nonstick cooking spray. Pound chicken breasts to ¼ inch thickness. Sprinkle each piece of chicken on both sides with salt and pepper. Place 1 cheese slice and 1 ham slice on top of each breast. Roll up each breast, and secure with a toothpick. Place in baking dish, and sprinkle chicken evenly with bread crumbs. Bake for 30 to 35 minutes or until chicken is no longer pink. Remove from oven, and place ½ cheese slice on top of each breast. Return to oven for 3 to 5 minutes or until cheese has melted. Remove toothpicks, and serve immediately.

Faye Jameson

Chicken Stew

Whole chicken
2 diced tomatoes
1 med sliced onion
1 small whole onion
1/2 pkg baby carrots
6 - 8 small red potatoes
1 pkg sliced mushrooms
Red, green, yellow, or orange pepper strips (optional)
2 stalks celery diced
1 stalk celery cut in half
1 - 2 Tbsp flour
1 c water

Rinse cavity of chicken in cold water. Salt & pepper cavity. Stuff with whole onion and celery stalks. Salt & pepper outside of chicken. Add all ingredients to dutch oven. Bake at 325 degrees for about 30 - 40 minutes per pound of chicken. Chicken should be almost ready to fall off the bone. Remove chicken and vegetables with slotted spoon. Mix flour with small amounts of water to make a thin paste. Heat pan drippings over low heat. Slowly add thin flour paste to drippings while stirring. Add more to achieve desired consistency. Pour over chicken and vegetables.

Note: If using a roaster chicken, this can be done in a crock pot, low heat for 8 - 10 hours, or on high for 4 - 5 hours.

Linda Kidwell

Cornish Game Hens with Wild Rice

4 Cornish Game Hens
Uncle Bens Wild Rice (original not fast cooking)
1 c orange juice
1 c pancake syrup

Cook wild rice according to directions. Rinse cavity of hens. Salt & pepper cavity. Stuff with rice. Tuck wings under bird. Place in baking dish, breast side up. Salt & pepper to taste. Bake at 325 degrees for about 45 minutes. Combine orange juice and syrup. Pour over birds. Bake an additional 1/2 hour or until done. (legs will move up & down easily)

Linda Kidwell

Holiday Cranberry Chicken

1 can whole berry cranberry sauce
1 pkg. Lipton Onion soup
1 8 oz bottle French Dressing

Mix and spoon over 5 to 6 boneless chicken breasts. Bake uncovered for 1 ½ hours at 350 degrees. Serve with wild rice.

Sharon Tynan

Hot Chicken Salad

1 can Cream of Chicken soup
½ c mayonnaise
3 Tbsp lemon juice
½ tsp salt
¼ tsp pepper
3 c diced chicken
½ c sliced almonds
2 Tbsp onion flakes or diced onion to taste
1 c sliced water chestnuts
3 hard cooked eggs, cubed
2 c bread crumbs

Mix all ingredients together except crumbs, put in 7 x 11 baking pan or casserole. Top with crumbs. Bake at 350 for 20 to 30 minutes until bubbly.

Sandy Sabbagh

Lasagna

1 lb Italian sausage
1 clove garlic
½ tsp basil
1 ½ tsp salt
1 lb can tomatoes
2- 6 oz cans tomato paste
10-12 lasagna noodles
2 eggs
3 c cottage cheese
½ c parmesan cheese
2 Tbsp parsley
½ tsp pepper
1 tsp salt
1 lb mozzarella cheese

Brown meat and drain. Add garlic, basil, salt, tomatoes and tomato paste. Cook noodles in salted boiling water until tender, but not done. Rinse and drain. Beat eggs and add cottage cheese, parmesan cheese, parsley, pepper and salt.

Make layers in a 9x13" pan layering as follows:
1) Noodles
2) Egg & cottage cheese mixture
3) Meat sauce
4) Mozzarella cheese
Repeat layering

Bake at 375 degrees for 30 to 40 minutes.

Can make ahead, but may take longer to bake if it has been refrigerated overnight.

B.J. Blankenfeld

Maryland Crab Cakes

1 egg
4-5 slices of bread (state or lightly toasted)
Fresh parsley (use a good amount)
2-3 tsp dry mustard
Salt and pepper
3-4 heaping Tbsp mayonnaise (okay to use low-fat or light)
1 lb Back fin crabmeat (fold in last and try to maintain lumps)

Mix all ingredients together. Makes 6-8 crab cakes depending on the size. Sauté quickly in hot canola oil. Add a little bit of Old Bay seasoning. Place crabcakes on dish with several paper towels to absorb any extra oil.

Darlene Cook

Meat Loaf

2 lb ground beef
1 pkg dry onion soup mix
2 eggs
¼ c brown sugar
2/3 c quick oats
½ c milk
4 Tbsp Ketchup
3 Tbsp Mustard

Mix all ingredients and shape into loaf in glass baking dish. Cover top and sides of meat loaf with ketchup. Bake at 350° for 1 ½ - 2 hours.

Shauna Williams

Miso-Marinated Sea Bass

4- 6 oz Sea Bass Filets
¼ c white miso paste
¼ c sake
¼ c mirin
2 tsp soy sauce
¼ tsp sesame oil

Place fish in dish large enough for fish to lay flat. In a large bowl whisk together all remaining ingredients. Pour over fish, turn to coat. Cover and allow to marinate in refrigerator for 30 minutes turning occasionally. Can be broiled or grilled on high, 4-5 minutes per side, turning only once. Start with skin side up.

Shannon Passwaiter

Sloppy Joes

1 lb lean ground beef
¼ c chopped onion
¼ c chopped green bell pepper
½ tsp garlic powder
1 tsp yellow mustard
¾ c ketchup
3 tsp brown sugar
Salt and pepper to taste
6 hamburger buns

In a medium skillet over medium heat brown the beef, onion and green pepper; drain. Stir in the garlic powder, mustard, ketchup, and brown sugar; mix thoroughly. Reduce heat and simmer for 20-30 minutes. Season with salt and pepper. Serve on buns.

Faye Jameson

Southern Style Deep Fried Chicken

6 chicken thighs or drumsticks
3 c evaporated milk
1 tbsp + 1 tsp salt
3/4 c all purpose flour
1 tsp cayenne pepper
1 egg beaten

Place chicken in large Ziplock bag add milk. Refrigerate at least 2 hours or overnight. Transfer chicken into large saucepan. Add milk. Bring to a boil. Reduce heat to medium low allowing chicken to simmer until chicken is cooked through entirely, about 20 minutes. Remove chicken from milk and place on rack to cool. Allow to sit until warm, about 15 minutes. Pat dry. Heat vegetable oil in Dutch oven or deep fryer to 325 degrees. In a large zip lock bag, add salt, cayenne pepper, and flour. Shake to combine. In a medium bowl, beat 1 egg. Place each piece of chicken, one at a time, in bag and shake to coat. Dip chicken in egg. Place chicken back in bag to coat a second time. Repeat with each remaining piece. Gently drop each piece into hot oil, allowing the skin to crisp and turn brown, about 1 minute per side. Remove from oil and transfer to a paper towel lined plate. Serve immediately.

Linda Kidwell

Stuffed Green Peppers

1 lb ground beef or chuck
1 lb ground pork sausage, preferably Italian style
1 15 oz can crushed tomatoes
1 5 oz can tomato paste
¼ tsp fennel seeds
¼ tsp Italian seasoning
¼ tsp salt
¼ tsp black pepper
3-4 cups cooked rice
4 large green peppers halved and cleaned
1 8oz can tomato sauce

Preheat oven to 350 degrees.
In a large skillet brown ground beef and sausage; drain. Add tomatoes, paste, fennel, Italian seasoning, salt and pepper to skillet. Combine on medium low heat until heated through and fennel begins to release its flavor. Add cooked rice to your liking. This changes the density of the filling. I usually go with about 3 cups cooked. Place green pepper halves in lined 9x13 baking dish. Scoop filling into pepper halves. Drizzle can of tomato sauce over peppers once they are stuffed in pan. Bake covered for about 30 minutes. Uncover and bake for another 25-30 minutes or until green peppers are tender to your liking.

Faye Jameson

Texas Pot Roast

3 lb chuck roast
Water
2 Tbsp red wine vinegar
3 beef bouillon cubes
1 tsp chili powder
2 large onions, chopped
1 large green pepper, seeded & chopped
1 can (1 lb, 12 oz) chopped tomatoes for chili
1 can (16 oz) kidney beans for chili
Salt & pepper
1 c shredded Mexican style cheese
1 c chopped green onions
Tortillas or corn bread

Trim excess fat from roast. Place in 4-5 quart heavy metal pan along with 1/2 cup water. Cover and cook over medium high heat until meat releases juices and turns gray - about 30 minutes. Uncover. Cook juices away. Then turn meat in rendered fat until well browned on both sides, about 30 minutes more. Lift meat out and set aside To pan, add 1/4 cup water and the vinegar. Scrape pan to loosen browned bits. Add bouillon cubes, chili powder, onions , and green pepper. Cook, stirring, for about 10 minutes. Add tomatoes and their liquid. Add kidney beans. Stir to mix. Return meat to pan. Cover. Bake at 325 degrees for about 2 hours. Skim off fat. Add salt & pepper to taste. Serve hot. Garnish with cheese and green onions. Serve with tortillas or corn bread. Makes 4 servings.

Linda Kidwell

Venison Tenderloin

1 lb venison tenderloins (medallions)
½ tsp fresh ground pepper
3 medium onions (thinly sliced)
1 clove garlic (mashed and diced)
3 Tbsp butter
4 ounces mushrooms (fresh, sliced)
3 Tbsp flour
2 cups water
Salt

Lightly sprinkle tenderloins with pepper and set aside. Sauté onions in 1 Tbsp butter. Add garlic and cook another 3 minutes. Add mushrooms, sautéing another 10 minutes. When done, remove vegetables and add the rest of the butter. Sauté venison 2-3 minutes per side. When done, place on platter and return vegetables to pan. Add flour stirring until it becomes a thick brown paste. Add water, continuing to stir, until gravy is of desired consistency, adding more water if you wish. Correct seasoning and pour over tenderloins. Serve.

Patrick Casey

Pastries, Desserts, Cakes & Frosting

Apricot Crumb Bars

2 ¼ c all purpose flour
1 c sugar
1 c pecans (finely chopped)
2 sticks butter
1 egg
1 jar apricot preserves

Heat oven to 350 degrees. Spray 9x12 or 13" pan with Pam.

Combine flour, sugar, pecans, butter and egg in a bowl. Beat on low speed for 2-3 minutes scraping sides of bowl often. Mixture will be crumbly. Remove 2 cups of the mixture and set aside. Pour remaining crumbly mixture into pan pressing down firmly to form crust. Spread apricot preserves over crust within ½ inch of crust. Sprinkle remaining 2 cups of mixture on top. Bake 40 minutes or until lightly browned. Cool completely before cutting.

Barbara Joseph

Cake Dough Peach Dessert

Melt:
1 stick margarine or butter in 9 x 13 pan in oven.

Mix together:
1 c flour
1 c sugar
2 tsp. baking powder
¾ c milk

Beat together and pour on top of melted butter.

Pour:
1 large can sliced peaches and juice over batter. Bake at 350 degrees until crust is brown on top.

Marnise Bounds Miller

Caramel Apple Cake

1 Duncan Hines Carmel Cake mix
1 can apple pie filling (1 use Comstock's More Fruit)
3 eggs

For Topping:
1 pt container Marzetti's Caramel Apple Dip
Chopped peanuts

Mix ingredients and bake in 350 degree oven in greased and floured cake pan until done, usually about 45 minutes. Cake will stay dense and moist, but when it starts to pull away from the edges of the pan, it's done. Nuke Marzeti's Caramel Apple dip in microwave for a few seconds, stir, nuke again, and stir briskly until it's very spreadable. Dump on top of warm cake and smear to cover. Sprinkle with chopped peanuts or other chopped nuts of your choice (optional). Enjoy!

You can make this as a sheet cake or a Bundt cake. If you do it as a Bundt cake, it actually looks like the bottom side of a caramel apple that's been dipped in chopped peanuts. Kind of cute for a kid's cake, which is how it came to be invented in the first place.

Cindy Oswalt

Cheesecake(s)

Crust
1 stick butter
1 ½ c graham cracker crumbs

Preheat oven to 350°. Melt butter until very hot, add graham cracker crumbs and combine. Spread on the bottom of a 9" spring form pan. Bake for 10 minutes. Turn oven down to 225°.

Filling
2 ¼ pounds cream cheese
1 c sugar
5 eggs

Bring cream cheese to room temperature, or warm up in microwave. Add to mixing bowl and whip with sugar until light and fluffy. Add eggs one at a time, scraping bowl two or three times. Pour into spin form pan and bake in 225 degree oven for 2 ½ hours. Top with 1 c whipping cream sweetened with 1 Tbsp sugar. Whip until cream forms soft peaks.

Lemon cheese cake; add ½ c lemon juice and 2 Tbsp lemon zest

Berry cheesecake; add 2 c raspberries, strawberries, blackberries, blueberries, or mixed berries. Frozen fruit without sugar added is fine.

Pumpkin cheesecake: 1 15 oz can pumpkin. 1 Tbsp cinnamon, 1 tsp nutmeg, 1 tsp cloves

Mocha Chocolate Chip cheesecake; 1 c strong espresso, 1 Tbsp, cocoa, 1 c chocolate chips (add half prior to putting cheesecake in oven, then add half about 45 minutes prior to removing from oven).

Cappuccino cheesecake; 1 c strong espresso and 1 Tbsp cinnamon

Becky Wann

Chocolate Fudge or Icing

1 c sugar
1 Tbsp cocoa
1/3 c evaporated milk
½ stick margarine or butter
½ tsp vanilla

Mix sugar and cocoa together. Then add milk and butter. Mix well and boil 1 ½ minutes for icing and 2 minutes for fudge. Remove from heat and stir in vanilla. Set pan in cold water and stir until mixture begins to thicken and loose it's shine. Add nuts if desired.

For Fudge: Pour onto a buttered dish and let cool.

Marnise Bounds Miller

Chocolate Glaze

2 Tbsp Butter
2 Tbsp Cocoa
2 Tbsp Water
½ tsp Vanilla
1 c confectioner's sugar

Melt butter. Add cocoa and water. Stir constantly until thickened. DO NOT BOIL. Remove from heat and add vanilla. Gradually add confectioner's sugar, beating until smooth.

Becky Wann

Clafouti

3 c blueberries (rinse)
2 Tbsp candied ginger
¼ c plus 1 Tbsp sugar
1 c low fat milk
3 eggs
½ c flour
2 tsp vanilla extract
Block chocolate shaved-dark or bittersweet

Preheat oven to 325°

Butter a deep 10 inch pie plate or shallow baking dish. Arrange blueberries and ginger in the bottom of the plate and sprinkle with ¼ c of sugar. Pour milk into a blender and add eggs, flour, vanilla and remaining sugar. Blend on high until mixed, 1 minute. Pour butter directly from blender over the fruit in the plate. Bake for 25-30 minutes or until or until clafouti is lightly browned on edges. Top with shaved chocolate cut into 6 pie-shaped wedges and serve warm.

Mary Ann Kiko

Crisco Pie Crust

For single 9 inch crust
1 1/3 c flour
½ tsp salt
½ c Crisco
4 Tbsp cold water

Combine flour and salt in a mixing bowl. With a pastry blender, cut in Crisco until uniform; mixture should be fairly coarse. Sprinkle with water, a little at a time; toss with fork. Work dough into a firm ball with your hands. Roll out on floured surface until desired size. Place in pie pan. Fill with filling of your choice and bake accordingly.

Marnise Bounds Miller

Crock Pot Cake

1 (18 oz) chocolate cake mix
¾ c oil
1 (3 oz) instant chocolate pudding
4 eggs
2 c sour cream
1 c water
1 (8 oz) pkg. chocolate chips

Spray pot lightly with oil spray. Mix all ingredients. Pour into pot. Cover. Cook on low for 7 hours only. Spoon into bowls. Top with Cool Whip or serve alone.

Patt Spahn

Derby Pie

1 c chocolate chips
1 c chopped pecans
2/3 c sugar
½ c flour
1 stick melted butter (cooled)
1 tsp vanilla

Mix all ingredients in large bowl. Pour into frozen deep-dish pie crust. Bake 1 hour at 325 degrees or until crust is golden brown.

Barbara Joseph

Divine Apple Strudel

¼ c apple juice
½ c golden raisins
2 to 3 Granny Smith or Gala apples (about 1 pound); peeled, cored, halved and thinly sliced
½ c lemon, juiced
1 Tbsp lemon zest
1 tsp ground cinnamon, plus more for sprinkling
½ c brown sugar, packed
¼ c chopped pecans
2 Tbsp butter, melted for brushing onto phyllo sheets, plus more if needed
1 Tbsp granulated sugar
Confectioner's sugar
Glaze:
2 c confectioners sugar
3 ½ Tbsp. milk
For the glaze: Mix ingredients together thoroughly
For the strudel:

Preheat the oven to 350 degrees F. Line a baking sheet with parchment paper. In a small bowl, pour apple juice over the raisins and microwave on high for 45 seconds. Let sit for 15 minutes. Next combine the raisins, apples, lemon juice, lemon zest, cinnamon, brown sugar, pecans and butter in a large bowl. Remove the phyllo dough from the box, unfold, and cover with a damp towel. Place 1 sheet of phyllo on the work surface and brush lightly with melted butter. Repeat with the remaining sheets, brushing each with melted butter, stacking when done, being sure to keep the unbuttered phyllo covered.

Place the apple mixture on the nearest third of the phyllo stack, being sure to leave a 2-inch border. Gently lift the bottom edge of the phyllo stack to cover the filling and fold the side edges over. Continue to roll the stack away from you until the filling is completely sealed in and the seam is on the bottom. Transfer to the prepared baking sheet. Brush the top with butter and sprinkle with granulated sugar. Bake for 30 minutes, until golden brown. Pour Glaze over and sprinkle with confectioner's sugar.

Andrea Reeves

English Coffee Cake

2 c brown sugar
3 c margarine
2 eggs
¼ c coffee (liquid)
½ c Muscat Raisins (can substitute large golden raisins)
1 c chopped walnuts
3 c flour
1 tsp baking soda

Boil raisins until tender. Drain. Mix together brown sugar, margarine, eggs. Mix in coffee. Add flour, soda, raisins, and nuts. Bake in 9 x 13 pan for 10 to 12 minutes. Then cook in 5 minute intervals, checking doneness by inserting toothpick in center. It is done when toothpick comes out clean.

Linda Kidwell

European Fudge Sauce

¾ c cocoa
¾ c granulated sugar
½ c light brown sugar packed
dash salt
¾ c whipping cream
½ c softened butter
1 tsp. vanilla
Chopped Nuts (optional)

Mix all ingredients together. Serve over ice cream

Becky Wann

Grand Marnier Chocolate Cake

1 chocolate cake mix
1 chocolate instant pudding mix
4 eggs (extra large)
½ c cold water
½ c canola oil
½ c orange juice
Zest of 2 oranges, finely chopped (about 2 Tbsp)
1 c pecans

Preset oven to 325 degrees F. Grease and flour one Bundt cake pan or three 2-pound cake tins. Mix all ingredients except pecans for 2-3 minutes on medium speed of electric mixer, scraping sides of bowl as needed to incorporate all ingredients. For Bundt cake, sprinkle pecans even over bottom of Bundt pan. If baking 2# cakes, stir pecans into batter. Pour batter in baking pan(s). Bake for 45-55 minutes or until cake tests done. Let cake cool thoroughly—overnight is best, if you can manage to wait until morning to glaze. Remove the Bundt cake from the pan and put on serving plate. Just leave the pound cakes in the pans.

Glaze
¼ pound of butter
¼ c water
1 c sugar
½ c Triple Sec
Grand Marnier, to taste

Heat butter, water, and sugar in a heavy saucepan over moderate heat until mixture is boiling. The entire surface of the liquid should be bubbling up a storm. Cook, stirring, for 5 minutes. Remove from heat. Add Triple Sec. Stand back when you do this. The liquor will get an enthusiastic reception. Ladle over cake(s). Sprinkle top of cake with Grand Marnier as desired. (I tried adding Grand Marnier to the glaze, but the consistency of Triple Sec works better.) Cover tightly with aluminum foil or plastic wrap. Let steep for 24 hours, if you can wait that long. Enjoy!

Becky Wann

Green Slime Dessert

First Layer

1 c flour
½ c margarine
½ c finely chopped pecans

Combine and mix thoroughly. Pat into 9" x 13" pan. Bake 15 minutes at 350 degrees. Cool completely

Second Layer

8 oz pkg softened cream cheese
1 c powdered sugar
1 c Cool Whip
Mix together. Spread on first layer. Chill

Third Layer

2 pkgs instant pistachio pudding
3 c milk
1 tsp vanilla

Beat until thick and pour over second layer

Fourth Layer

Top with Cool Whip and sprinkle with chopped pecans. Chill thoroughly.

Linda Kidwell

Joan's Coffee Cake

½ c oleo
3 eggs
2 c sifted flour
1 tsp. baking soda
1 tsp. baking powder
½ tsp. salt
1 c sugar
1 c sour cream
1 tsp. vanilla

Cream eggs butter and sugar. Combine flour, baking soda and baking powder in separate bowl. Combine sour cream and vanilla. Alternate adding flour mixture and sour cream mixture until everything is combined.

1 c chopped walnuts
¾ c brown sugar
1 tsp vanilla
2 tsp. butter

Pour ½ of the batter in a greased tube pan. Sprinkle with half of the nut mixture. Pour remaining batter in tube pan and top with the remainder of the nut mixture. Bake at 350 degrees for 50 minutes.

Faye Jameson

Miracle Whip Cake

1 c sugar
1 c Miracle Whip
3 – 4 Tbsp. cocoa
2 c cake flour
2 tsp baking soda
Pinch of salt
1 tsp vanilla
1 c warm water

Mix together sugar, Miracle Whip, and cocoa. Sift together flour, baking soda, and salt. Combine. Add vanilla and water. Bake in greased 8 x 12 pan at 350 degrees for 18 – 20 minutes.

De Ann Wright

Moist and Easy Cookie Sheet Chocolate Cake

2 c sugar
2 c flour
2 sticks butter
1 c water
4 Tbsp. cocoa
½ c buttermilk
1 Tbsp. baking soda
1 Tbsp. vanilla
2 beaten eggs

Mix together sugar with flour. Set aside. In a small pan, bring the butter to a boil. Add water and cocoa. Pour over sugar/flour mixture. Add buttermilk, vanilla, and eggs. Mix well and pour onto greased and floured cookie sheet that has a rim. Bake at 400 degrees for 20 minutes. Dust with 10XX sugar or frost with fudge frosting.

Sandy Sabbagh

My Favorite Chocolate Frosting

1 ¼ c semi sweet chocolate chips
½ c strong coffee
6 oz softened butter

Melt chocolate with coffee. Add butter. Mix until consistency is a little thicker than pudding.

Becky Wann

One Egg Cake

1 stick butter
¾ c sugar
1 ¼ c flour
1 tsp. baking powder
1 egg
½ c milk
1 tsp. vanilla

Cream together butter and sugar. Add other ingredients in order given. Pour into a greased 8 x 8 pan and bake at 350 degrees until done. Recipe can be doubled to make a 9 x 13 sized cake.

Marnise Bounds Miller

Pineapple Carrot Cake

2 c all-purpose flour
2 c sugar
1 tsp baking powder
1 tsp baking soda
1 tsp ground cinnamon

Combine above ingredients Add:

3 c finely shredded carrots

1-8 ¼ oz can un-drained crushed pineapple
½ c coconut
1 c cooking oil
4 eggs

Beat all ingredients until combined. Pour into 2 well-greased and floured 9 x 1 ½ round pans. Divide it into 3 layers. Bake at 350° for 40 minutes until toothpick inserted in center comes out clean. Cool on wire rack for 10 minutes, then remove from pans.

Remember to spray the heck out of your pans with PAM (I mean A LOT), and to use the flour.

Gloria Yeary

Poppy Seed Cake

1 c poppy seeds
1/3 c honey
1/3 c water
1 c butter
1 ½ c sugar
4 eggs, separated
1 tsp. vanilla
1 c sour cream
2 ½ c flour
1 tsp. baking soda
1 tsp. salt

Preheat oven to 350 degrees.

Grease and lightly flour a 9" tube or bundt pan. Combine poppy seeds, honey and water in saucepan. Bring to a rolling boil and continue to cook for 4 - 5 minutes. Turn heat down and simmer for another 2 minutes. Cool. Cream butter and sugar until light and fluffy. Add poppy seed mixture. Add egg yolks, one at a time, beating well after each addition. Blend in vanilla and sour cream. Sift flour, baking soda, and salt together. Gradually add to poppy seed mixture, beating well after each addition. Beat egg whites until stiff. Fold into batter. Pour batter in pan. Bake for 1 hour and 15 – 20 minutes. Cool for 5 minutes in pan. Remove from pan and cool on a baking rack. Frost with cream cheese frosting.

Becky Wann

Pumpkin Spice Cake

¾ c butter
1 ½ c firmly packed brown sugar
3 eggs
1 ½ c pumpkin
3 c sifted cake flour
¾ c baking soda
½ tsp salt
1 ½ tsp cinnamon
¾ tsp nutmeg
¾ tsp Allspice
¾ tsp ginger
¾ c Buttermilk
Chopped Nuts

Preheat oven to 350 degrees.

Butter and flour a bundt pan.

Cream butter and sugar until light and fluffy. Add eggs, one at a time, beating well and scraping bowl after each addition. Add pumpkin and mix. Stir together dry ingredients. Add to batter alternately with the milk. Beat 2 minutes on medium speed, then fold in chopped nuts. Bake 45 minutes. Cool in pan 15 minutes, then invert onto a cooling rack. Frost with cream cheese frosting.

Becky Wann

Strawberry Pie

1 ½ c flour
½ c powdered sugar
1 ½ sticks margarine, softened
8 oz cream cheese, softened
1 can Eagle Brand Condensed Milk
1 tsp vanilla
1/3 c lemon juice
1 qt strawberries (sweetened to taste)
4 Tbsp corn starch
Cool Whip

Mix flour, powdered sugar, and margarine together. Spread on pizza pan. Bake at 350 degrees for 20 minutes. Allow to cool completely before adding next layer. Mix together cream cheese, Eagle brand milk, vanilla, and lemon juice. Spread on cooled crust. Bring strawberries, corn starch, and sugar (if desired) to a boil. Reduce heat and cook until clear, stirring frequently. When cool, spread over cream cheese layer. Top with Cool Whip

Shannon Passwaiter

Strawberry Pizza

1 ½ c flour
½ c powdered sugar
1 ½ sticks margarine, softened
8 oz cream cheese, softened
1 can Eagle brand milk
1 tsp vanilla
1/3 c lemon juice
1 qt strawberries (sweetened to taste)
4 Tbsp corn starch
Cool Whip

Mix flour, powdered sugar and margarine together and spread on pizza pan. Bake at 350 degrees for 20 min. Allow to cool completely before adding next layer. Mix together cream cheese, Eagle brand milk, vanilla and lemon juice. Spread on cooled crust. Bring to boil, strawberries, corn starch and sugar (if desired). Reduce heat and cook until clear stirring frequently. When cool, spread over cream cheese layer. Top with Cool Whip.

Shannon Passwaiter

Tami's Praline-Pumpkin Cake

½ c butter
¼ c whipping cream
1 c packed brown sugar
¾ c coarsely chopped pecans
1 pkg Betty Crocker Super Moist Yellow Cake Mix
1 c canned pumpkin (NOT pumpkin pie mix)
½ c milk
1/3 c vegetable oil
4 eggs
1 ½ tsp. pumpkin pie spice
1 container cream cheese frosting
Caramel topping
Chopped pecans

Heat oven to 325°

Stir butter, cream, brown sugar – cook over low heat, stirring occasionally just until butter is melted. Pour into 2 round cake pans, sprinkle evenly with ¾ cups pecans. Beat cake mix, pumpkin, milk, oil, eggs and 1tsp. pumpkin pie spice with electric mixer on low speed until moistened. Beat 2 minutes on medium speed. Carefully spoon batter over pecan mixture in each pan. Stir 1/2tsp. pumpkin pie spice into frosting. Place 1st cake, praline side up, spread with half of the frosting. Repeat with 2nd cake. Drizzle caramel topping and pecans over cake.

Annette Lower

Turtle Brownies

For Batter:
1 German chocolate cake mix
1/3 c evaporated milk
¾ c melted butter (Don't think about it)
1 c chopped nuts (you can use pecans)

For caramel:
1 14 oz bag caramels
1/3 c evaporated milk
For yumminess:
1 c semi-sweet chocolate bits

Preparation:
Unwrap and melt caramels with milk in bowl in microwave, stirring briefly every couple of minutes to facilitate melting. Keep warm. IN mixer, or with spoon, blend cake mix, butter, and milk until well-mixed. Batter will be very thick. Stir in nuts. Using back of spoon, a spatula or fingers, pat half of batter into bottom of 9" x 13" baking pan (you can use metal cake pan with a cover, so it makes for easy storage). Don't worry it you can't get it to spread evenly. Just try for a minimum of bare spaces. Bake in 350-degree oven for 6-8 minutes. You don't want to let it get too dry, but you don't want it all mushy, either, or you'll never get the brownies out of the pan. Remove pan from oven and immediately sprinkle chocolate bits over top of batter, and drizzle caramel mixture over those. Then, drop remaining cake batter by spoonfuls on top of caramel. Bake for 16-18 more minutes. Batter will have risen, but brownies are best if you take them out of the oven before they are too thoroughly baked and let them fall. Very nice and chewy that way! Enjoy!

Cindy Oswalt

Velvet Frosting

1 stick butter or margarine
1 c sugar
2/3 c milk
6 Tbsp. Crisco
3 heaping Tbsp. flour
1 Tbsp. vanilla

Beat butter and Crisco together until softened. Add sugar and beat well. Add flour, one tablespoon at a time, beating well after each addition. Beat in milk, then vanilla. Beat until sugar is melted and the frosting is like whipped cream.

Marnise Bounds Miller

Vermont Maple Walnut Pie

¾ c granulated sugar
½ c firmly packed brown sugar
1/3 c softened butter or margarine
3 eggs
½ c light cream
¼ c maple syrup
¼ tsp salt
1 and ½ c broken walnuts
1 tsp vanilla
9 inch unbaked pie shell

Oven 350°, In a saucepan, cream the sugars and butter. Add the eggs and beat well. Add the cream, maple syrup, and salt and cook over low heat for 5 minutes, stirring constantly. Remove from heat and stir in walnuts and vanilla. Pour into pie crust and bake about one hour. Makes one pie.

Sharon Tynan

Walnut Carrot Cake

1 ½ c walnuts
1 c oil
3 c sifted flour
1 ½ tsp. cinnamon
3 tsp. baking powder
1 tsp. nutmeg
1 tsp. salt
¼ tsp. cloves
2 c packed brown sugar
3 Tbsp. milk
4 lg eggs
3 c grated carrots

Chop ½ cup walnuts fine. Grease 3 (9 inch) layer cake pans well. Sprinkle each with about 2 ½ Tbsp. Finely chopped walnuts to coat. Chop remaining walnuts a little more coarsely and set aside. Re-sift flour with baking powder and salt. Combine sugar, oil, eggs, and spices. Beat at high speed until light and well mixed. Add half of four mixture; stir until well blended. Add milk, then remaining flour. Stir in carrots and chopped walnuts. Divide batter evenly in pans. Bake at 350 F. for 25 minutes until cakes test done. Let stand on wire racks 10 minutes. Turn cakes out onto wire racks to cool. When cooled, frost with a butter cream frosting. Decorate with walnut halves. Makes 1 large cake, 12 servings.

Sandy Sabbagh

Weinerbrod Danish Pastry

1 c cold milk
1 egg
10 Cardamom seeds or ¾ tsp. Ground Cardamom
1 pkg dry yeast
2 Tbsp sugar
¼ c warm water
½ tsp. salt
3 c flour
1 c softened butter

Sprinkle the yeast over the warm water and let stand 10 minutes. Add beaten egg, milk, ground cardamom, sugar, and salt. Mix well and add the flour. Work into a dough until stiff enough to handle. Place the dough on a floured board and roll into a rectangle. Spread the entire surface with the softened butter. Fold together sides and ends over the center. Repeat this 6 times, spreading with butter each time. Place in refrigerator for 2 hours. Roll out, cut with a doughnut cutter and twist. Place on a greased cook or jelly roll sheet. Let rise at least 30 – 45 minutes in a warm room. Bake at 400 degrees for about 8 minutes. Frost with a fairly thick frosting made with confectioner's sugar and a small amount of milk or cream with a drop of vanilla. Serve warm.

Joyce Wilson

Yummy Quick Chocolate Cake

2 c sugar
2 c flour
1 tsp baking soda
1 tsp salt
1 stick butter
½ c vegetable shortening
1 c water
1 tsp vanilla
6 Tbsp cocoa
2 eggs
½ c milk
2/3 c walnut or pecan pieces (Nuts are optional)

In a large bowl put sugar, flour, baking soda & salt. Melt butter & vegetable shortening then stir in coca, then add water. Pour on to flour mixture and beat until smooth. Add slightly beaten eggs and milk and mix thoroughly. Add vanilla and mix. Pour in jelly roll pan with 1" to 1 ½ " sides or cookie sheet. Bake at 400 degrees for 20 minutes. While the cake is cooking prepare the icing. Once prepared immediately after the cake comes from the oven pour the icing on top and spread evenly. Can be eaten immediately!!! Delicious!!!

Yummy Quick Chocolate Cake Icing

1 stick butter
3 c powdered sugar (small box)
7 Tbsp milk
1 tsp vanilla
4 Tbsp cocoa

Melt butter, stir in cocoa then add milk. Bring to a boil then stir in powdered sugar until smooth. Add vanilla & nuts. Pour on top of the cake & enjoy!!

Pat Figg

Soups, Salads, & Sauces

Antipasto Salad

Head of chopped iceberg lettuce
Small can of tuna, drained
Layer of sliced pepperoni
Layer of prosciutto
Layer of sliced salami
Jar of artichoke hearts, drained
Layer of mozzarella (grated or sliced - your choice)
Can of black olives, drained
Small jar of green olives, drained
Grape tomatoes
Sprinkle with freshly grated Parmesan cheese
Garnish with pepperocini

Top with Italian Dressing or a Vinaigrette

Linda Kidwell

Asian Cole Slaw Salad

2 pkgs beef Ramen noodles
1 c slivered almonds, toasted
1 bunch green onions
3/4 c vegetable oil
16 oz slaw mix
1 c sunflower seed kernels
½ c sugar
1/3 c white vinegar

Remove noodles, crush and put in bottom of bowl. Add slaw, almonds, sunflower seeds and green onion in layers. Whisk together oil, vinegar, sugar and seasoning packets from noodles. Pour over slaw. Chill for 24 hours. Toss and serve.

Alice French

BBQ Sauce

1 bottle Heinz Ketchup (don't know why, but it has to be Heinz to come out right)
1 1/2 Tbsp vinegar
1 tsp liquid smoke (use more according to tastes)
1 cup brown sugar

Combine all ingredients. Add additional brown sugar if too thin. Keeps well in refrigerator until you're ready to use it.

Linda Kidwell

Bean Salad

Mix together:
1 can yellow wax beans
1 can French style green beans
1 can kidney beans, drained
1/2 c green pepper, chopped
1/2 c celery, chopped
1/2 c diced onion

Then add:
1 c sugar
1/2 tsp each salt and pepper
1 Tbsp water
3/4 c vegetable oil
1/2 c vinegar

Mix well and refrigerate

Marnise Bounds Miller

Broccoli Cauliflower Salad

Mix in large bowl:
1 head cauliflower, broken into bite size pieces
1 bunch broccoli, broken into bite size pieces
1 red onion, sliced & cut into small pieces
1 block cheddar cheese, cubed

In a medium bowl mix:
½ c sugar
1 c mayonnaise
Touch of cider vinegar (to taste)
Bacon bits (optional)

Mix dressing ingredient and pour over vegetables and cheese. Dressing will be thick. Let set overnight and it will be very creamy.

Brenda Badger

Broccoli Slaw Salad

1 pkg Broccoli Slaw
1 bunch scallions, tops included, sliced
1 pkg Raman Noodles, crushed

Sauté ½ c sunflower seeds in 2 Tbsp butter or margarine
Combine and set aside

DRESSING:
3 Tbsp Sugar
3 Tbsp wine vinegar
¼ c olive oil
½ tsp salt
¼ tsp pepper

In a small jar, mix dressing ingredients and add the flavor packet
from the noodles to the dressing. Pour dressing over slaw and serve immediately so noodles will be crunchy when eaten.

Sandy Sabbagh

Chicken and Hominy Soup
(Posole')

3 boneless chicken breasts
3 small cans of white hominy
½ chopped yellow onion
1 dry bay leaf
2 pressed garlic cloves
1 chicken bullion cube
12-14 cups of water

Boil chicken breasts in a large pot for 20 minutes. Remove chicken and cut into cubes, put back in pot. Add hominy (drained) and stir in remaining ingredients above. Simmer on low for 25 minutes.

Serve in bowls and sprinkle with the following:
- a. Mix 2-3 chopped fresh jalapeno peppers, ½ chopped onion, 6-8 sprigs of diced cilantro.
- b. Slice 4 limes into wedges.
- c. Chop ½ cabbage (finely chopped as if for cole slaw).

Serve in bowls and sprinkle with the following:
- d. Mix 2-3 chopped fresh jalapeno peppers, ½ chopped onion, 6-8 sprigs of diced cilantro.
- e. Slice 4 limes into wedges.
- f. Chop ½ cabbage (finely chopped as if for cole slaw).

Pat Harth

Chicken Noodle Soup

Whole chicken or leftovers work (you can also use the leftover turkey carcass)
Small package frozen mixed vegetables
Package of frozen egg noodles
1 diced onion
1 diced stalk of celery
1 box chicken stock
Water
Salt & Pepper

Rinse cavity of chicken. Place in large kettle or soup pan. Add chicken stock. Add water until chicken is covered. Add onion, and celery. Bring to boil. Lower heat to simmer for 1 ½ to 2 hours or until chicken is falling off the bone. Remove chicken. Let cool. Remove bones. Place meat back in pot. Bring to boil. Add vegetables. Add noodles and cook according to directions. (Additional stock & water can be added if needed for noodles to cook) Season with salt & pepper according to taste.

Linda Kidwell

Chili

1 lb. Ground Round or Sirloin
1 Small Onion Chopped
1 - 8 oz can Tomato Sauce and 1 can of water
1 - 10 oz can Ro-Tel Diced Tomatoes w/Green Chilies
1 - 14 oz can Red Gold Petite Diced Tomatoes w/Green Chilies
1 - 30 oz can Brooks Chili HOT Beans

Brown ground beef and onions, drain well and return to skillet or Dutch oven. Add tomato sauce, can of water, all tomatoes, chili bean. Stir well and let simmer on medium low heat until heated through. If you prefer more spice, add some Mexene Chili Powder and/or some Ground Red Chili Powder.

Other additions:
Macaroni or spaghetti.
Can be topped with cheese, sour cream, Fritos. Enjoy!
If you like it soupier, just add another can of water. If you have a food processor or blender, you can blend all of the tomato products together for less chunky chili.

Serves 4-6 people.

Connie Rautenkranz

Crab Salad

Mix together the following:

1 pkg of chopped artificial crab
3-4 chopped green onions (green included)
1/4 c chopped celery
3-4 Tbsp mayonnaise
1 Tbsp lemon juice

Linda Kidwell

Raising Dough

Cranberry Salad

Grind:
1 pkg cranberries and add ½ c sugar – let sit overnight

Next day add:
1 box cherry Jell-O
½ pkg small marshmallows
1 c drained, crushed pineapple
½ c pecans chopped
Mix & chill (looks very pretty in a crystal dish)

DeAnn Wright

Egg Salad

8 hard boiled eggs
¾ c mayonnaise
¼ tsp paprika
¼ tsp white pepper
½ tsp dill weed
2 Tbsp capers
2 Tbsp chopped sweet roasted peppers
2 Tbsp chopped fresh chives
2 Tbsp Dijon mustard

Combine all ingredients except eggs and mix. Grate eggs into bowl and combine. Chill.

Becky Wann

Gazpacho

1 #5 can diced tomatoes (28 oz)
1 ½ c tomato juice
1 ½ c water
1 ½ c finely chopped onion
1 ½ c finely chopped celery
1 ½ c chopped green pepper
1 cucumber or zucchini, peeled, seeded and diced
¼ c finely chopped fresh jalapenos
¾ tsp salt
¾ tsp hot sauce

Combine all ingredients and chill.

Best if allowed to marinate for a day or so.

Becky Wann

Great Split Pea Soup

1 pkg split peas & water
Salt & Pepper to taste
3 bay leaves
4 beef bouillon cubes
4-5 parsnips
3 leaks
2 Tbsp butter

Wash and cook split peas according to directions. Add salt, pepper, beef bouillon cubes and bay leaves to peas. Peel parsnips and chop in small pieces. Wash leaks thoroughly and chop in small pieces. Cook parsnips and leaks in butter in microwave until tender. Add to peas for the last hour of cooking time.

Lu McDonald

Lentil Vegetable Soup

2 c dry lentils
2 slices diced bacon
½ c chopped onion
½ tsp oregano
½ c chopped celery
1 lb canned, crushed tomatoes
½ c chopped carrots
2 Tbsp wine vinegar
3 Tbsp snipped parsley
1 clove minced garlic
¼ tsp pepper
2 ½ tsp salt

Rinse lentils. Drain, and place in soup kettle. Add 8 cups of water and remaining ingredients except for tomatoes and wine vinegar. Simmer covered for 1 ½ hours. Add tomatoes and vinegar. Simmer covered for 30 minutes longer. Season to taste.

Brenda Badger

Lemon Chicken Artichoke Soup

1 lb cooked, diced chicken breast
1 stick of butter
1 c diced onion
½ c diced red pepper
1 clove of minced garlic
½ tsp ground pepper
salt to taste
2 c chopped artichoke hearts
1 c flour
2 c of Weiss or blonde ale
6 c chicken broth
½ c lemon juice
¼ c fresh chopped tarragon or dill
2 c cream

Melt the butter in a stock pot and sauté the vegetables until they soften. Add seasonings and stir in the flour. Wisk in the ale, broth and lemon juice. Bring to a simmer until it thickens, add chicken, parsley and cream, adjust the salt.

Fred Manion

Mandarin Almond Spinach Salad

Dressing:
½ c canola
1/3 c Splenda sugar (not the packets)
5 Tbsp white vinegar
1 tsp salt
1 ½ tsp minced dry onion
1 ½ tsp poppy seed

Salad:
1 bunch spinach washed very well
1 c celery, sliced
½ c (+/-) green onion
1 can mandarin oranges or more
8 oz mozzarella cheese, cubed or more

Almonds:
½ c slivered almonds sautéed very slowly in 2 Tbsp sugar. Cool & break apart.

Garnish:
Mandarin oranges
6-8 oz cubed mozzarella cheese
Almonds

Directions:
1. Combine dressing ingredients & refrigerate early in the day.
2. Prepare almonds watching very closely as they burn quickly.
3. Place spinach in salad bowl & add celery & green onion on top. Cover with saran wrap and refrigerate until ready to serve.

Mix and serve in small dishes with garnishes sprinkled over salad.

Gloria Yeary

Mandarin Orange Salad

1 head of red leaf lettuce
1 large can of mandarin oranges, drained
1 small pkg chopped walnuts

Combine ingredients
Top with poppy seed dressing

This is also good substituting fresh, sliced strawberries, and almonds with a raspberry vinaigrette dressing.

Linda Kidwell

Meat Marinade

1 1/2 c vegetable oil
3/4 c soy sauce
1/4 c Worcestershire sauce
2 Tbsp dry mustard
1 tsp pepper
1/2 c wine vinegar
1 1/2 tsp dried parsley
1/3 c lemon juice

Combine all ingredients. Marinate meat 24 - 48 hours. Especially good with London Broil cut.

Linda Kidwell

Oriental Cabbage Crunch Salad

2 Tbsp sesame seeds
1/2 c slivered almonds

Toast in oven or toaster oven until golden

1/2 head finely shredded cabbage
4 chopped green onions
1 pkg Ramen chicken flavor
1 breast roasted chicken, cut in small chunks

In a large bowl combine: cabbage, chicken, onions, almonds, sesame seeds, and broken up Ramen noodles (not cooked, but broken into very small pieces).

Dressing
Combine the following in a jar:
2 tsp sugar
1/2 c oil
3 Tbsp rice wine vinegar
1/2 tsp salt
1/2 tsp pepper
1/2 pkg of the Ramen seasoning

Shake well. Toss with salad. Serve immediately

Linda Kidwell

Pat's Ham and Bean Soup

1 (8 oz) bag of raw pinto beans
1 ham bone or ham hock
1 c diced ham cubes
½ finely chopped bell pepper (optional)
½ chopped red onion
2 minced garlic cloves
¼ c of Worcestershire sauce
1 dry bay leaf

Clean and rinse beans with water, removing any debris.
Soak beans in large bowl for two hours but can be soaked overnight if refrigerated.
Drain water from beans and place beans in large crock pot with other ingredients.
Add water to about ½ inch from top.
Set crock pot on low for 8 to 10 hours.

Remove bay leaf and serve in medium sized bowls with slice of corn bread.

Pat Harth

Potato Salad

6 potatoes
1/2 c chopped onion
1/2 c chopped celery
4-6 Tbsp mayonnaise
2 Tbsp yellow mustard

Boil potatoes until fork tender. Soak in cold water for about 20 minutes (this makes them easier to peel). Dice into bite size pieces. Add remaining ingredients. Sprinkle top with paprika. Chill overnight.

Linda Kidwell

Potato Soup

4 cooked potatoes, peeled and cubed
1 medium diced onion
2 slices bacon
stalk of celery, chopped
salt & pepper
Tarragon
3 c Half & Half Milk/Creamer (use more for thinner consistency)
Instant mashed potatoes
1 Tbsp Flour

Cook bacon with celery and onion until bacon is crisp. Add flour to renderings to make a paste. Add milk slowly, stirring to combine. Add potatoes. Season with salt, pepper, and tarragon to taste. Add mashed potatoes to thicken to desired consistency. Cook over very low heat for at least 2 hours.

Linda Kidwell

Salsa Cruda

1 14 oz can diced tomatoes
1 14 oz can crushed tomatoes
½ can water
1 lg onion, diced
2 tsp salt
3 cloves garlic, minced
2 Tbsp olive oil
1 tsp cayenne

Sauté onion and garlic in oil in saucepan until onion is translucent. Add tomatoes and water. Simmer for twenty minutes. Good with cheese enchiladas or chile rellenos.

Becky Wann

Salsa Ranchera

3 Tbsp Flour
¼ c oil
¼ c chili powder
1 Tbsp cumin
1 Tbsp paprika
2 c beef or chicken stock

Brown flour in oil, add spices and toast for about 2 minutes stirring constantly. Add broth and bring to a boil. Boil for about 3 minutes, then reduce and simmer for 15-20 minutes. Good for beef or chicken enchiladas.

Becky Wann

Salsa Verde

2 ½ lbs tomatillos
1 – 2 jalapenos, depending on preference
2 poblanos
1 qt water
1 tsp sale
½ bunch cilantro

Clean tomatillos. Clean, remove stems and seed peppers, then chop coarsely. Bring all ingredients to a simmer and simmer for 15-20 minutes. Please in blender.

For cold salsa verde for dipping, follow same recipe except only use 1 cup water and do not cook.

Becky Wann

Sesame Dressing

1 can Hoisin Sauce
1 jug honey (microwaved)
¼ c ginger
¾ c chili paste
1 can Hiosin Soy Sauce
2 c water
1 qt lime juice
1 bunch cilantro, chopped
1 bunch green onion, chopped
4 c blended oil
1 c sesame oil

In a large stainless bowl, whisk together Hoisin, honey, ginger & chili paste until well mixed. Measure soy in Hoisin can ½" from top. Whisk in with water & lime juice. Add cilantro & green onion. Whisk in oils last. Whisk until well blended. Store in two 8 qt. containers.

Lennie's Restaurant

Spaghetti Sauce

1 lb ground Italian sausage
1/3 green pepper, chopped
1/3 yellow pepper, chopped
1/3 red pepper, chopped
1/2 lg red onion, chopped
1/2 tsp chopped garlic
8 oz pkg fresh, sliced mushrooms (portabella is a good choice if available)
1 lg can generic spaghetti sauce
1/2 tsp Italian seasoning
1/2 tsp oregano
1/2 tsp basil
1/2 tsp crushed red pepper
Freshly grated parmesan

Lightly brown sausage in large kettle. Add peppers and onions. Cook slowly until peppers are almost tender. Add mushrooms and garlic. Cook slowly until mushrooms are tender. Add sauce and seasonings. Seasonings can be adjusted to taste. Cook slowly for at least 1 hr (2-3 hrs is better). Serve over spaghetti and top with parmesan.

Linda Kidwell

Sweet – Savory Salad

Salad:
1 bag fresh baby spinach
1 bag fresh spring greens mix, or lettuce of choice
1 can drained mandarin oranges
Sliced almonds

Dressing:
½ c brown sugar
½ c salad oil
1/8 c vinegar or lemon juice
¼ c finely chopped onion
¼ tsp salt
¼ tsp paprika
1/8 tsp dry mustard
1/8 tsp red pepper flakes

Wisk together dressing ingredients. Pour over salad just before serving. If dressing is too thick add a small amount of warm water. Serves 6 – 8.

Jill Weber

Tuna Salad

4 cans white tuna packed in water
3 hard boiled eggs
½ cup finely chopped onion
½ cup finely chopped celery
¾ cup mayonnaise
1/3 cup pickle relish
2 tsp dried tarragon
½ tsp ground white pepper
1 tsp lemon zest
¼ tsp salt

Drain tuna. Grate eggs. Combine all ingredients in a bowl and chill.

Becky Wann

Tuna Salad

Mix the following together:

Lg can of tuna in water, drained
1/4 cup chopped onion
1/4 cup chopped celery
1 Tbsp. sweet pickle relish (hot pepper relish is good in this also, but use 1/2 as much)
3 Tbsp mayonnaise (use more if too dry)

Linda Kidwell

Vegetable Soup

1 small bag frozen mixed vegetables
4 - 6 c water
1 small can diced tomatoes
1 large can tomato juice
1 small can tomato sauce
1/2 head chopped cabbage
Soup bone or cubed chuck
pickling spice

Add all ingredients except pickling spice in large dutch oven or soup pan. Cover with water. Put pickling spice in spice ball or tea ball. Hang over side of pan, making sure it's immersed in liquid. Cover. Cook over low heat 3-4 hours.

Linda Kidwell

Veggie Chili

Serves 6   30 minutes total time to make
5 ½ c water
¾ c bulgur wheat
2 tsp. olive oil
1 c chopped onion
1 c chopped red pepper
2 Tbsp salt-free chili powder
2 tsp. minced garlic
2 tsp. ground cumin
1 can (28oz) crushed tomatoes
1 can (15oz) 100% pure pumpkin
1 medium zucchini, diced
1 c frozen corn
1 can (15.5 oz) low-sodium black beans, rinsed
½ c chopped cilantro
Garnish: reduced-fat sour cream & reduced-fat cheddar cheese

Put 3 cups of the water and the bulgur in a medium microwave-safe bowl. Cover and microwave on high until bulgur is tender, about 15 minutes. Meanwhile, heat oil in a large soup pot and add onion and pepper and sauté 5 minutes. Add zucchini and sauté. Add chili powder, garlic and cumin; sauté until fragrant. Add remaining 2 ½ cups water, the tomatoes, pumpkin, and corn; bring to boil over medium-high heat. Reduce heat and simmer 10 minutes, stirring occasionally, until vegetables are tender. Stir in beans and bulgur; heat through. Remove from heat and garnish individual bowls with cilantro, sour cream and cheddar cheese.

Andrea Reeves

Wanda's Cranberry Sauce Extraordinaire

1 c water
1 c white sugar
1-12 oz package fresh cranberries
1 orange, peeled, cored, and diced
1 pear, peeled, cored, and diced
½ c dried blueberries
½ c dried apricots, chopped (6oz)
1 c chopped pecans
½ tsp salt
1 tsp cinnamon
½ tsp nutmeg

Directions:
In a medium saucepan, boil water and sugar until the sugar dissolves. Reduce heat, add all ingredients. Cover and simmer for 30 minutes, stirring occasionally, until the cranberries burst. Remove from heat and let cool to room temperature.

Special Notes:
Since you can only get fresh cranberries around the holidays, it makes a great holiday side dish. If you can't find dried blueberries, just use package mixed dried fruit.

To make 6 times this recipe. It's a piece of cake to make a larger batch. Just be sure to start with a larger pot. After it cools to room temperature, put it in pint freezer containers. Thaw in the refrigerator and enjoy all year long.

Kit Holland

The Perfect Kitchen

Tips for the Perfect Kitchen!

By Jennifer Courtney
Pampered Chef Consultant

As a young girl, I used to pull my chair up to the counter and help my mother prepare and cook meals for the family. That time was so special to me to be able to have my Mother's undivided attention. What I didn't realize is that I was learning valuable secrets and lessons that have helped me growing up in the kitchen, and even more so now that I'm a Pampered Chef Consultant!
The Perfect Kitchen needs a FEW necessities!

•First off is Cookware! Now whether you're a Stainless Cookware user or a Hard Anodized, getting the RIGHT cookware is critical to your cooking needs in your kitchen. Good Cookware will keep you from burning food, cooking unevenly, which promotes over done and under done food, and can determine a good meal from a bad one!

What to look for in GOOD Stainless Cookware! Tri-ply is the key ingredient in Stainless for even cooking. Typically an aluminum core is surrounded by a grade of Stainless steel. Aluminum heats VERY hot but is flimsy—so when it's sandwiched between two sheets of stainless, you get a premium-cooking compound. A brushed Stainless on the interior allows for easy clean up. Hollow Handles keep your from burning your fingers, so look for handles that are solid at the base, and then hollow so you can pick up your pans off the stove without oven mitts. Flared rims are very important if you ever want to pour out liquids. This will keep it from dripping down the side.

What to look for in GOOD Hard Anodized! Hard anodized cookware is the easiest to clean and therefore one of the most popular choices in cookware. Look for a Coating that has been applied more than once and baked into the pan to keep it from flaking up and putting "pepper" in your food. A titanium reinforcement in the cookware aids to durability and long life. Look for flared rims again, and for handles wrapped in silicone.

•Another MUST have is GOOD CUTLERY! A good knife will help you "slice time" out of your cooking! Quality knives are constructed to be FULL TANG. That means that the metal goes from one end of the knife to the other. It's not just down to the handle and then glued in. A good multipurpose knife is a Santoku. Santoku knives have the Grantons on the knife, which help release sticky foods as you slice them such as Potatoes. The highest quality knife is made of German Forged Steel. This process starts with a piece of metal that is heated, hammered and cooled to promote flexibility and durability. A Super Sharp edge and a good piercing tip will complete a well-crafted knife. Maintaining that sharp edge by honing frequently and professionally sharpening is mandatory. Once a good quality knife is used, you'll NEVER use another!

•A good Cutting Board is almost as important as your knives! A good cutting board absorbs the blade of the knife, but does not harbor Bacteria. Polyethylene and Polypropylene are excellent cutting surfaces that will accomplish just that, and as a bonus is dishwasher safe. Always use different cutting boards to cut your meat from your vegetables so as not to contaminate your food. Never cut on glass as it is a very dense surface that will chip and dull your knives horribly!

• Good Baking Sheets are a must for baking delicious cookies, breads, pizzas and pastries! Of course as a Pampered Chef girl, I would have to recommend STONEWARE as the ultimate Baking sheet. Stoneware absorbs excess moisture from your food, making it virtually impossible to burn. It heats and cooks evenly, doesn't warp in the oven, and maintains temperature for around 30 minutes so you can consume warm pizza from slice one to slice 8! It's the easiest to clean as it gets "seasoned" as it cooks like Cast Iron. PERFECT results EVERY time is what you can expect, and no longer relying on the "Smoke-d-timer" as your timer :o)

• Lastly, a Good Mixing Bowl Set is essential for the Perfect Kitchen. A set of 3 or 4 sizes for every need you may have is a good idea. A good mixing bowl can be glass or stainless, with a deep well for mixing, and possible a gripping attachment on the bottom to keep it from moving all over when you're mixing your food. A good set would have 2, 4, 6, and 8- quart capacities, and would be even better if they have seal down lids.

There are many more items that could be included in this list—but these are critical items for the Perfect Kitchen.

THE WELL EQUIPPED KITCHEN
Information was obtained from The Food Network website.

Pots and Pans

The kind of pots and pans you buy depends on your own personal preference. Generally, stainless is the most versatile, though both hard-anodized and nonstick have their fans. Look carefully at cookware sets — while they're often a great deal, they may not include exactly what you need. Our ideal set-up includes:
* 9-inch omelet pan
* 12-inch skillet
* 8-quart stockpot with a lid
* 1.5-quart sauté pan with a lid
* 1.5-quart saucepan with a lid
* 3-quart saucepan with a lid

In addition to that, you might want the following:
* 9-inch cast-iron skillet
* Roasting pan and rack
* Ridged grill pan
* 5-quart Dutch oven
* Steamer insert for saucepan
* Casserole dish

The Right Tool for the Right Job

A well-equipped kitchen makes cooking easier and more fun. Here are our recommendations for:

Knives:

When you're buying a knife, the most important thing is how it feels in your hand. If you're particularly enamored of a certain style of grip, then buying a block is your best option; if you prefer a different grip for different styles of knife, then purchase your knives individually.

* Paring knife
* Serrated knife
* Chef's knife (either French-style or Asian)
* Carving/Slicing knife
* Kitchen shears

Utensils and Equipment:

Utensil-wise, the kind of pans you have dictate the kind of utensils you should be using. Nonstick pans demand plastic utensils; wood and metal can be used on hard-anodized and stainless pans.

* Cutting boards (ideally more than one)
* Spoons (regular, slotted, and wooden)
* Metal spatula (sometimes called a turner)
* Rubber spatula
* Can opener
* Box grater
* Rasp grater
* Pepper mill
* Vegetable peeler
* Whisk
* Tongs
* Instant-read thermometer
* Salad spinner
* Colander
* Ladle

Small Electronics:

* Blender (stick or countertop)
* Food processor
* Toaster or toaster oven
* Microwave
* Slow cooker
* Pressure cooker
* Mixer, handheld or stand

Baker's Goods:

If baking is your passion, consider adding the following:
* Two (9-inch) cake pans
* Mixing bowls
* Measuring cups and spoons
* Cookie sheets (both rimmed and flat)
* Cooling rack
* Spring form pan
* Pastry brush
* Rolling pin
* Loaf pan
* Pie pan
* Removable-bottom tart pan

Pantry

Keep these items on hand for easy meal preparation.

Spices (Basic):
* Kosher Salt
* Whole black peppercorns
* Red pepper flakes
* Dried herbs, like oregano, bay leaf, whole nutmeg, and thyme
* Ground cinnamon
* A spice blend such as
* Chili powder
* Curry powder
* Herbes de Provence or Italian Seasoning
* Five-spice powder

Spices (Upgrade):
* Ground cumin
* Ground coriander
* Paprika
* Fennel seeds
* Ground cardamom
* Allspice

Condiments (Basic):
[all of these go in the fridge once open]
* Ketchup
* Mustard
* Hot Sauce
* Jelly

* Salsa
* Soy sauce
* Worcestershire sauce
* Real maple syrup

Condiments (Upgrades)
* Asian chili pastes
* Sesame oil
* Fish sauce
* Hoisin sauce
* Chutney

Dry goods (Basic):
* Vegetable oil
* EVOO
* Vinegar
* Chicken broth (canned or in paper containers)
* Nut Butter
* Honey
* Pasta
* Canned tomatoes
* Rice
* Whole Grains, such as:
* Oatmeal, Bulgur
* Canned Beans

Dry goods (Upgrade):
* Polenta
* Couscous
* Canned chilies (pickled jalapenos, chipotles in adobo)
* Jarred anchovies
* Tomato paste
* Bread crumbs

Baking:
All-Purpose Flour
* Baking Powder
* Baking Soda
* Sugar (White & Brown)
* Vanilla extract
* Chocolate Chips

About the Authors

The Bloomington Board of REALTORS® (BBOR) is a professional trade association representing REALTORS® in Monroe and Owen Counties, Indiana. Chartered in 1947, BBOR maintains affiliations with both the National and Indiana Associations of REALTORS®, and the many institutes, societies and councils that offer professional accreditation to its members. BBOR and its members maintain at the core of their activities the REALTOR® Code of Ethics, the first of its kind among professional trade associations. BBOR is the sole shareholder of its two subsidiary companies, Bloomington MLS, Inc. and BBOR Publications, Inc. Members of Bloomington Board of REALTORS® are committed to the community in which they work and live. The BBOR's volunteer standing committees include the American Red Cross Blood Drive Committee, the Food Drive Committee to help "Feed the Kids", Jill's House Committee that presents the annual "Home for the Holidays Tour", Salvation Army Bell Ringing Committee, and the annual Toy Drive Committee. In addition, the BBOR Community Grant Committee distributes budgeted funds to local charities and provide hours of community service. BBOR also annually contributes to Habitat for Humanity.

BLOOMINGTON BBOR
BOARD OF REALTORS
Working together. Working for you.

Printed in the United States
129842LV00002B/1-6/P